1984

University of St. Francis
GEN 301.435 A646
App, Austin Joseph,
Making the later years count:

T4-ALA-711

MAKING THE LATER YEARS COUNT

MAKING THE LATER YEARS COUNT

For a Healthy, Well-Provided, Blessed Old Age

AUSTIN J. APP, Ph.D. ASSOCIATE PROFESSOR OF ENGLISH LANGUAGE AND LITERATURE, LA SALLE COLLEGE, PHILADELPHIA, PENNSYLVANIA

THE BRUCE PUBLISHING COMPANY
MILWAUKEE

LIBRARY
College of St. Francis
JOLIET, ILL.

Library of Congress Catalog Card Number: 60–16965

© 1960 THE BRUCE PUBLISHING COMPANY
MADE IN THE UNITED STATES OF AMERICA

301.435
Q646

112,342

TO

MY MOTHER

Who, Active and Vigorous at Seventy-eight,
Is Making the Later Years Count,
Temporally and Spiritually.

Preface

THE inexorable alternative of life is that one must either die young — or get old. The pathos of life is that one gets old before one realizes it, or is ready for it. As the Pennsylvania Germans put it, "We grow too soon old / And too late smart." The Old Testament promises long life to the good. But long life is a blessing only for those who can make the later years count.

The key to a joyous and fruitful old age is sincerely accepting it. To make the later years count, to make them blessed for ourselves and for others, one must accept the fact of growing old in the light of God's purpose. The German priest-philosopher, Romano Guardini, in a radio address entitled, "The Evening of Life," said rightly:

> What first and decisively has to be said, on which indeed the whole wisdom of life must be founded, is that only he grows old in the right way who sincerely accepts his growing older.
> (Munich, Germany, Dec. 28, 1956)

This book tries to make it easier to accept the fact of growing older and of being old. It is intended to help prepare for the later years and to make them count, materially and spiritually. It calls upon whatever in science, sociology, and religion can guide us to and through the later years wisely, on all counts: physically, economically, socially, and above all spiritually.

Science and better living habits are increasing the life span steadily — especially in America, Canada, and Western Europe. In 1900, only 4.4 per cent of Americans were over 65; in 1955, almost double that percentage were over 65. Now that some fifteen million people in the United States are over 65, which is one in twelve, a widespread interest in gerontology has developed.

But my own interest in the phenomenon of aging can be said

to date to boyhood. It started, somewhat unhappily, when a bearded gentleman, rocking on a porch, on our first meeting enthralled me with his tale of the old Wild West, but on my second visit distressed and bored me by retelling not only the same tale but telling it seemingly word for word. A few years ago, recalling that incident, I began an article on the conversational hazards of old age. It grew into two: one, somewhat philosophical, entitled, "Old Age as a Spiritual Opportunity" (*The Catholic World*, Apr., 1954), the other, directed more to my original purpose, entitled, "Happy Oldsters Sidestep Their Pitfalls" (*The Holy Name Journal*, Oct., 1954).

Other articles followed: "Where and What People Live Longest" (*Nord-Amerika*, Aug. 14, 1958); "Sands of Gold: Poets prepare us to accept old age" (*Magnificat*, Jan., 1959); "The Catholic Stake in the Aged" (*Social Justice Review*, Jan., 1959): and, "Are Grandparents Appreciated?" (*Magnificat*, Sept., 1959). These articles brought me the invitation to act as a consultant on the workshop, "Programs for the Aged," during the convention of the National Council of Catholic Men (Detroit, Apr. 4, 1959). As often happens, though I thought at first to satisfy with a few articles my preoccupation with the topic, the resultant correspondence and encouragement enlarged and deepened my interest in growing old to the point of writing a book.

Here is the book. There are many and excellent other books on the later years. Since, as Samuel Johnson averred, ". . . a man will turn over half a library to make one book," I have seen and read a good many of these (to some of which I will refer from time to time). Like every author, I feel indebted to all those who wrote on the topic before me, both for contributing information and for promoting interest in it. If then, despite the quantity and high quality of previous books on old age I add one of my own, it is partly because among the scores of books, only perhaps two are Catholic and not widely known.

But most of all, I feel, what any author should feel if he is to write at all, that I have a point to make, a special insight to contribute. I want to portray the blessedness of the later years, their unique gift as a spiritual opportunity, their precious capacity as a bridgehead between this life and the next. I want people to feel that old age is not so much a problem as an opportunity — a golden one for weaving all the loose ends of one's life together into a holy cord with which to swing into the bliss of heaven.

I want to set down all the material aids for a creative and contented old age, but even more, the spiritual needs and resources with which to keep our sights always firmly fixed on the final end and purpose of it all. I want to make people embrace old age rather than dread it. I want to help them, even should theirs be an old age of sorrow, sickness, and pain, still to see God's beneficent purpose in it and feel its Christian blessedness.

Upon finishing a book manuscript on a serious topic intended for the general reader, one feels keenly how much one owes to so many scholars and investigators past and present. Many of them spent a lifetime, sometimes little recognized and less rewarded, in laboratories and libraries bit by bit advancing man's knowledge to the point where a general book can be written. Though they cannot well be named, I pay them my deep-felt tribute.

As to my own sources, scholarly and popular, I confined them in general to publications of the past five or six years. I have tried in all cases to give credit in adequate references, inserted as part of the text rather than as footnotes. The bibliography and index, too, are meant to be helpful rather than formal and exhaustive.

In addition to the information from published sources, I am also indebted for some to Georgine E. Bowen, Harried Bury, and Alice Dashiel, members of the Philadelphia Division of Health; to Msgr. Thomas J. Rilley, Director, and Sister Margaret Loretta of the Philadelphia Catholic Charities; and to several of my colleagues at La Salle College, most particularly Mrs. Georgette M. Most, Reference Librarian, who besides giving me the customary assistance of a librarian, alerted me to several geriatric events and publications. Mrs. Else Loos, my cousin, sent me

helpful material from Munich, Germany; Mrs. G. Parr, from
Washington; and Father Clarence D. White, from St. Louis.
Valuable advice and encouragement came also from many friends
and relatives, especially from Anthony N. Ries, M.D., of Philadelphia — who while I was writing the last chapters also allevi-
ated my gout; and my sister, Mrs. Martina Wagner, R.N., M.A.,
Upper Mont Clair, New Jersey, with whom I discussed my outline
and the details of some of the chapters. Most of all, I am indebted to Editor Aloysius Croft, of The Bruce Publishing Company, for encouraging the project from the beginning.

A. J. App

September, 1960

Contents

MAKING THE LATER YEARS COUNT

CHAPTER I

The Later Years: A Spiritual Opportunity

ROBERT FROST, the venerable New England poet, is credited with the story in which, in answer to the question, "Why does grandmother read the Bible so much," a youngster pipes up with, "She's probably cramming for her final exam!" This anecdote epitomizes the high purpose of man's later years.[1]

When all the poets and the gerontologists — those who occupy themselves with the study of the phenomena of old age — have had their say, the crucial truth about the later years is that they give us an invaluable chance to get our spiritual house in order, to doff more and more of the natural man and don the supernatural one. It is the privileged time, after the sweat and toil of the occupational years, to get ourselves spiritually spruced up for the not-too-distant moment when we hope to enter into the kingdom of heaven on the arm of our Guardian Angel. It is a proper time of prayerful anxiety *lest* we fail to make ourselves worthy enough in the numbered years left to us.

Heaven is the place of which, according to St. Paul's inspired words,

> Eye has not seen nor ear heard,
> Nor has it entered into the heart of man,
> What things God has prepared for those who love him
> (1 Cor. 2:9).

And the wholesome fear of our unworthiness would be balanced by the realization that the worst is over — of trials and temptations — and the truly best, if we love God enough, is

---

[1] Some of the material in the early pages of this chapter has previously appeared in the author's article, "Sands of Gold," *Magnificat*, Jan., 1959.

"just around the corner." If, indeed, it could realistically enter into our hearts how blissful heaven is, how our whole reason for being born and living is to make ourselves worthy of heaven and finally to enter it, and if we could really *feel* what we must and do *believe* about the bliss of heaven, then we would welcome growing old, rather than fear it.

If we really felt, as many saints manage to do, that this life is merely a preparation and a prelude to the next, just as the years of college are the preparation for a vocation, we would not dread old age any more than the collegian dreads his senior year. We rightly consider anyone immature and imbued with wrong values who would delay rather than welcome his senior years and *Commencement*. In a true and even literal sense, the later years are the climax of our training for our supernatural *Commencement*, for the true vocation for which we were born: the eternal enjoyment in heaven of the beatific vision.

But while we are wrapped up in this "mortal coil" of ours, we cannot *feel* most Christian truths and mysteries the way we can believe them, and therefore we incline to the fear of old age. This fear we must try to moderate even though we cannot entirely conquer it. With the help of our Faith, and of right reason and the arts and sciences, we can convert our natural fear of old age into a sufficient anticipation of heaven to make the latter years not only endurable but creative and interesting.

The proper Christian spirit requires our acceptance of old age, for the fear of it can be a petrifying thing. In pre-Christian times, it drove many of the old pagans to suicide. Indeed, the Latin poet Juvenal called "Old age more to be feared than death." It is only Christianity that can logically convert the fear of old age into gratitude for the spiritual opportunity it provides.

But Christian logic does not automatically produce a Christian acceptance of old age. Francois Mauriac, in *Woman of the Pharisees*, presumably having a Christian woman in mind, wrote, "No one has written of the torment that old age brings to women of a certain type. In it they taste of Hell before death touches them." Nor do all men welcome old age in a genuine Christian spirit. Charles Dickens so dreaded old age that he dyed his hair and beard, replaced aging friends with younger men, and called himself the elder brother of his children rather than their father. His fellow novelist, William Henry Hudson, according to *Authors Today & Yesterday*, "had an intense dislike of dated events, for the reason (it is said) that he connected them with age and death . . . he habitually lied about his age."

A news feature on the inclusion of names in *Who's Who* revealed that,

> Major figures have had their small vanities. Andrew Mellon reduced his age by three years between Vols. 10 and 15. Henry Adams kept advancing his birth until a younger brother protested on the grounds of biological impossibility (*Inquirer*, Nov. 5, 1958).

Growing old is clearly repugnant to the Old Adam (and Eve) in us, to the natural man limited to this natural world. All the help of religion, science, and the arts is needed to aid us to accept old age in the wholesome Christian way. It is no easy project, for nature dotes frantically on youth and shrinks from age. "Nature," wrote Emerson, "abhors the old." The darkening cloud on every young horizon is the certainty that the so-called "best years of one's life" won't last even long enough to get used to them. While, as both Cicero and Swift pointed out, everyone wants to live long, everyone fears getting old!

But in order to make possible a fruitful and blessed old age, this natural fear of it has to be converted into a wise and real acceptance. As Father Romano Guardini said, ". . . all of life's true wisdom is founded" on the fact "that only he grows old the right way who deep within himself accepts his growing old." Old age is not the termination of life after which nothing comes; it is rather the proving time for the beginning of the life eternal. The later years, therefore, have a profound purpose of their own. They are a special privilege and should be accepted fully for what they are. They need to be so accepted if they are to bring their soul-saving blessings.

Most of us can easily imagine that for living saints, who have voluntarily gone on mortifying their flesh, old age, even one of illness and deformity, holds little dread and much hope. What needs to be emphasized is that ever for average Christians the later years tend quite naturally to be far more happy than they anticipated. In that stage they will probably feel like exclaiming with Andrew Lang, "Life's more amusing than we thought." All the worldly reasons which forecast a condition of misery mysteriously prove themselves fallacious. The later years tend to be far happier for most people than they had expected because God's reasons for old age are the true reasons, and the worldly reasons, phony. Paul Claudel wrote:

> I have now reached the days of which Ecclesiastes has very mistakenly said that they please me not. On the contrary they please me very much, and a man of sixty-three needs not to be reminded that light is sweet, and that it is delightful for the eyes to see the sun ("Old Age According to Sacred Scripture," trans. by Msgr. P. J. Doyle, P.P., *The Irish Ecclesiastical Review*, Oct., 1946).

Poets and sociologists tend to support Winston Churchill's comment on his seventy-seventh birthday that "we are happier in many ways when we are old than when we are young." Horace Walpole, British writer and statesman, who died at eighty, said, "Old age is no such uncomfortable thing, if one gives oneself up to it with a good grace." The most optimistic and best known, and yet also spiritually true, is Browning's, "Grow old along with me! / The best is yet to be, / The last of life, for which the first was made."

Longfellow in his "Morituri Salutamus," after declaring soberly, "Whatever poet, orator, or sage / May say of it, old age is still old age," nevertheless affirms strikingly and correctly that

> age is opportunity no less
> Than youth itself, though in another dress,
> And as the evening twilight fades away
> The sky is filled with stars, invisible by day.

The stars of age, invisible in youth, are the peace and contentment most sensible oldsters tend to experience. The secret of this contentment is probably the wisdom that comes from experience and from the ebbing of the sensual passions, *concupiscence,* as the theologians call it. The sobering, soothing growth of wisdom in the later years is well described and explained by the poet Edmund Waller, who lived to be 81 and published this when he was 79:

> The soul's dark cottage, battered and decayed,
> Lets in new light through chinks that time has made;
> Stronger by weakness, wiser men become,
> As they draw nearer to their eternal home.

The way and the privilege of the later years could not be described better.

The poets have tried to suggest the contentedness of a sensibly accepted old age by various analogies. Both Bacon and Scott analogized that since wood and wine improve with age, and friends and art, why should not we ourselves? John Townsend Trowbridge, author of "Darius Green and His Flying Machine," who died in 1916 at the age of 89, wrote, "With years a richer life begins, / The spirit mellows. / Ripe age gives tone to violins, / Wine and good fellows." Goldsmith, a year before his death at 46, in his *She Stoops to Conquer* has his elderly Hardcastle exclaim, "I love everything that's old — old friends, old times, old manners, old books, old wine."

Sociologists and gerontologists bear out the testimony of the poets that the later years should be contented and hopeful rather than dreary. Professor John T. Drake writes: "Basically, if a person is happy before retirement he is likely to be happy in retirement. Life before 65 will largely determine life after 65" (*The Aged in American Society,* Ronald Press, 1958, p. 134). Julietta K. Arthur, in *How to Help Older People,* writes:

> You need not steel yourself to endure old age, either in yourself, or in anyone else. A bouyant spirit can be retained till the end of life, provided the will is there. The capacity for love, for work, for intellectual enjoyment, for play — for a thousand other enjoyments — can endure, provided there is understanding and love to support them (J. B. Lippincott, Philadelphia, 1954, p. 70).

Dr. Nathan W. Shock in *Trends in Gerontology* (2nd ed., Stanford University Press, 1957) cites one survey as having "done much to dispel the belief that all older people are necessarily maladjusted invalids" (p. 155), and other studies as indicating that "with adequate preparation, retirement can be attractive to a good number of older people" (p. 137). Dr. Maurice E. Linden writes most encouragingly:

> The periods of maturity and later maturity possess the raw material out of which can be fashioned some of the most profound pleasures to which the human soul falls heir ("Preparation for the Leisure of Later Maturity," p. 97, in *Free Time*, University of Michigan Press, Ann Arbor, 1957).

In our later years very few of the things that mattered so much to us at twenty are around to worry and frustrate us. Friar Alfred Martin says that in the earlier years there is hardly ever a day when people "are not desperate about the outcome of some situation or issue or venture in their little lives" (*Friar*, Oct., 1958). In these earlier years, "money, fame, success, recognition, ability are prime values." To his list we add probably the most troublesome — romance! Later Friar Martin writes, these "lose their old importance . . . most of the transitory values disappear, and one has the feeling of being relieved of an intolerable load. . . . The usual cause of the desperation in the earlier years is false values," which in the later years tend to vanish.

It seems to me much of the secret of the surprising contentedness of the later years comes from this vanishing of false values, and perhaps the unconscious assumption of truer, more spiritual ones. Certainly many of our worst frettings and frustrations in youth, as we look back upon them, were largely due to false, transitory, and often even sinful values. We read of young people committing suicide because they failed relatively unimportant examinations or were jilted by their current boy or girl friend. Even a man as brilliant as the poet Willian Cowper, at thirty-two developed such a pitch of anxiety over an examination for a clerkship that he suffered the first of several recurring attacks of insanity.

When I tell my students, "You just do your work the best you can, and let me and the Holy Ghost worry about your grades," they groan unhappily that this is easily preached but not easily done. And they are right. Yet older people, who are in the process of substituting supernatural for natural values, are more easily able to do what they should and let God attend to the results. As Job said to Sophar the Naamathite, "In the ancient is wisdom, and in length of days understanding" (Job 12:12). Acquiring this understanding is the chance and privilege of the later years. Older persons can more easily follow Christ's very difficult advice, not to be solicitous for our life, what we shall eat, drink, or wear, for the Father knows of our needs. Peace and contentment are to be found in His injunction:

> Seek Ye therefore first the kingdom of God, and his justice, and all these things shall be added unto you.
> Be not therefore solicitous for tomorrow (Mt. 6:33, 34).

Rightly understood, these words contain the surest prescription for happiness ever spoken. They do not mean that we should sit on the wheelbarrow and wait for God to push it for us. They do not mean that we should not work for a living or store grain in the barn or money in the bank. They mean that we should do these things as well as we can — without worrying or fretting. We should indeed do our sensible earthly duty and do it with all our strength and talents — but we should trust the outcome humbly to God. We should feel that, win or lose, what God ordains is best for us.

But while our early passions are strong, our will unbridled, and our pride unbent, it is almost too much for the Adam in us to entrust the outcome of something we want so much and worked for so hard to anyone else — even to God! In the later years, however, after we have been buffeted through a long series of small victories and large disappointments, we can more gracefully bow to God's will. We will ruefully recall how things we

wanted, and got, turned out to be bad for us, whereas losses that
seemed heartbreaking proved lucky in retrospect. How can we
know that the one who broke our heart at twenty would not
have broken our spirit at forty! We simply cannot be sure that
what we want worldly-wise is really good for us or not — it takes
years to acquire this wisdom.

Oldsters whose life is anchored in Christianity find old age
generally quite tolerable. It is literally true that for them, "The
sky is filled with stars, invisible by day," because their body,
shorn of most of its concupiscence, "lets in new light through
chinks that time has made." This enlarged wisdom with the
years, this seeing through the glass, of which St. Paul speaks,
less and less darkly (1 Cor. 13:12) is both the privilege and the
duty of old age.

As we grow older, we must therefore make sure that we do
in fact grow in wisdom, that we accept the later years according
to God's design. The reward for doing so is the twofold one:
the later years will bring us incalculable spiritual blessings, and
they will prove enjoyable, or at worst, not insupportable.

Even physical infirmity and painful illness are endurable, as
countless saints have shown, if we can be resigned to them and
accept them as God's will for our spiritual good. Happily, modern
medicine has advanced to a point where some of the worst terrors
of pain and sickness need no longer be expected or dreaded.

Nevertheless, if we live long enough, it is probable that a
good deal of endurance will sooner or later be required of us
because of the very nature of our human existence. Samuel Johnson — for me a great Protestant saint — said, perhaps too pessi-
mistically, that "life protracted is protracted woe" and that
"Human life is everywhere a state in which much is to be endured, and little to be enjoyed." As we reach into the later years,
fewer and fewer pleasures stay with us, and more and more aches
and pains will seek us out.

But pleasures are not the substance of happiness, and saints
have found in the pangs of the stigmata the bliss of knowing
that their suffering was pleasing to our Lord — who Himself on

the Cross suffered much more for us than we could ever do for Him. If we pray resolutely for the grace to accept whatever our later years will bring and keep saying humbly and sincerely, "Lord, not mine but Thy will be done," we can assure ourselves of a successful old age — and probably a deliciously happy one. In the succeeding chapters, the specific factors of mind and body, health and wealth, joys and sorrows that make for well-adjusted and blessed later years will be recognized and developed.

CHAPTER II

Making the Most of Our Years

THE basis of contentment is the feeling that one has done the best one could under the circumstances. We tend to be content in the later years in proportion to our having made, and our actually making, the most of our years. To do so effectively we should start early measuring our plans and deeds against the yardstick of all our years — past, present, and the unknown but likely future ones. We should anticipate the latter wisely. We should try to get the various stages of life in true perspective early, take stock of our ultimate hopes and ambitions, and try to fit them sensibly into our likely span of years.

While we should seldom put anything fruitful out of our mind as too late, we should be even more on our guard against putting anything off as too early. If we want to get the most out of life, we must be up and doing from start to finish. Nature provides no coffee breaks for aimless dawdling. The lives of great men all give evidence of purposeful and unremitting activity; they amaze us by their indefatigable energy and zeal. They seem to know almost from youth what they want to accomplish — and steadfastly move toward it. In this, saints, scholars, and statesmen are alike.

But most of us of lesser stature, as we look back over our lives, have reason to reflect whimsically how the years stole upon us and caught us with many things never getting done which we had got in the habit of putting off. I quote with relish what one gentleman some years after his voluntary retirement wrote:

From youth to middle age the weeks, months and years pass slowly, one by one, almost unnoticed. A lifetime seems almost an eternity. We plan confidently, resolved to make our mark and fully realize all our ambitions. We're hardly conscious of or concerned with the passage of time. Even an indication of graying at the temples fails to warn us. Then, one day, suddenly, long before most of us have reached our goal, we come face to face with the cataclysmic fact that we are growing old (Theodore Groene, *How to Enjoy Retirement for the Rest of Our Lives* [New York, 1957], p. 36).

If we reflect, most of us will notice that as we approach the later years we keep shifting our perspective of what is young or old. While this lack of objectivity as to age tends to be amusing, it can also prove harmful. At least we should recognize it and allow for it. Until 21, people feel like upping their age; after that they tend to downgrade it. It is reported of one woman that she

gave her age on her first appearance in *Who's Who*, demanded that it be dropped in a later edition, and many editions later petitioned for its reinstatement because "I am now so old that my age is an honor" (Editorial, *Saturday Evening Post*, Apr. 29, 1939).

In one issue *Time Magazine* referred to Artist Artybasheff at 46 as middle-aged and to someone else at 42 as young. A reader agreed that 42 is young, but his neighbor's daughter, a late teen-ager, did not. The latter, on being told that her mother's friend at 42 was having a serious operation, offered as a consolation: "It doesn't particularly matter, Mother, if she doesn't pull through, she's so old anyway." *Time* commented that the "dividing line" keeps moving, and quoted the French as saying, "Forty is the old age of youth; fifty is the youth of old age" (Oct. 22, 1945). While the teen-ager's comment strikes us as amusing, we can also see how her false perspective on age is likely some score years later to land her in the later years unprepared and bewildered.

Most of us can probably remember our own false perspective as we revised upward the "dividing line" between what is young and what is old! At 23, arranging a blind date for a girl also about 23, I cautioned her that my friend was a bit old. Alarmed she asked, "How old?" When I replied, "Twenty-eight," she cried astonished, "Why, that isn't old!" Alas, with what embarrassment, and how often have I since recalled that false perspective of mine. In *Reader's Digest* (Oct., 1958), a woman related how, when as a teen-ager twenty years ago she saw the movie, *Mr. Skeffington*, in which the young heroine marries an older man for his money, she agonized over the plight of so young a girl being married to an old man. Recently, seeing the same movie again, she suffered once more, but this time it was "to see that chit of a girl behaving in such a despicable manner to that handsome, charming man."

Twenty-five years ago, when a girl, 24, was about to become engaged to a distinguished gentleman in his early fifties, I considered the age disparity perilous. But when in 1957 Bing Crosby, at 53, a widower with grown sons, married Kathryn Grant, 24, I felt unhesitatingly pleased about it. Reflecting an even greater shift in perspective, when T. S. Eliot, somewhat of an idol of mine, a widower of 69, married his secretary only 29, I shrugged the age disparity off with sympathetic ease!

The false perspective regarding age tends to work harm in two directions: in the early years we often put things off because we consider ourselves too young; in the later because we imagine ourselves too old. For those in the later years, the caution not to put things off out of youthful prodigality of time is hardly more practical than telling people that the best way to live long is to pick parents who lived long! But even for oldsters there remain many things which, like making their wills, they should not delay in doing.

"A man is not old until regrets take the place of dreams," said John Barrymore in our time; and Johnson long ago, "Life admits of no delays." Whether we are still young or already in the later years, we should lose no time — neither in vain regrets nor in faltering delays. We read that in 1926 F. Scott Fitzgerald called on Gertrude Stein and "said with energy":

Today is my birthday, I am 30 years old today. Thirty years old. Youth is over. What am I to do? What can I do? What does one do when one is 30 years old and when one's youth is over?

She told him, "Go home and write a novel, the novel that is in you to write. That is what you will do now that you are 30 years old." He did — and came up with *Tender is the Night* (*New York Times Book Review*, Mar. 3, 1951).

At thirty, at fifty, at seventy, and all the years between, there are things one can do, wants to do, or ought to do. With all the insistence I can bring to bear, I should like to tell everyone who has a deep-seated aspiration or ambition, "Somehow, someway, get started on it now. Find the time somehow — if only to scratch around the edges. But do at least peck away at what you really hope to do in your life." Whenever anyone seriously says, "Someday if I live long enough I will write — paint — carve — garden — fish — golf — collect this or that," whatever it is, if it is a deep-seated and worthy desire, he should find ways and means to get started on it immediately, at least in a small way, no matter how small!

As a matter of record, most of the people who make the kind of contributions to mankind that get inscribed in history books started on their specialty very early — in their twenties, even in their teens. We recall that Jesus at twelve, when His parents found Him amid the doctors in the temple, said to them, "Did you not know, that I must be about my Father's business?" (Lk. 2:49.) Writing this on the Fourth of July, I note that among the 56 signers of the Declaration of Independence, all already distinguished leaders, eighteen were still in their thirties, two in their twenties. John Hancock, the famous first signer, 39 at the time, had been elected to the Massachusetts Legislature at 29. Thomas Jefferson was only 33 when he wrote the Declaration; James Madison was 36 when he helped draft the Constitution; Alexander Hamilton was Washington's aide-de-camp at 20 and Secretary of the Treasury at 32. These men started early. Some decades later, Lincoln ran for the Illinois legislature at 25, and won; his adversary was Steven A. Douglas, only 23.

The giants in most areas not only continued long but started early. Edison, for example, who at 82 patented a process for making rubber out of goldenrods, had sold telegraphic patents at 22. In the realm of letters, which is my own major interest, most hands that mastered the typewriter started pounding it in their teens. Once preparing a talk on "High School Journalism — Key to Professional Writing" (Columbia Scholastic Press Assoc., Mar. 17, 1957), I was surprised to discover that many, perhaps most, noted writers had tried to write for publication before twenty. Longfellow, Marquand, Wouk, Merton, Santayana, for example, were published in their college magazines. Even more surprising is the large number who had written for their high school publications. One can cite Chesterton, Rupert Brooke, Adelaide Crapsey, and John Gunther. Bryant published one poem at 14 and wrote his immortal "Thanatopsis" at 16; Poe published *Tamerlane and Other Poems* at 18; and Hawthorne wrote his first novel in college and had it published at 24. Even Irving, who kept planning to be a lawyer but developed into a writer, had published his *Jonathan Oldstyle* essays before he was 20.

A further wealth of instances could be cited to show that if the tree is to incline a certain way, the sapling is wise to bend that way early. Many of those who make a pronounced success of something they ostensibly started late in life will be found to have had an avocational interest for many years previously. At a writer's conference, a man in his fifties told me he had sold out his business and was writing an historical novel about the time and events of the Revolution. Since he had never been published, I was skeptical of his either finishing the novel or getting it published so late in his life. But he did finish it, and while looking for a publisher, wrote a second one. After his first one was successfully published (*The King's Pardon*, Redman, London, 1958), I studied this mature achievement somewhat. I discovered that the author while a company executive had all along been collecting and reading books on the Revolutionary period which he used as background; and furthermore, that in his twenties he had written a complete, if unpublished, novel.

A similar policy is what I would strongly urge upon anyone who in the later years, after retirement perhaps, hopes to make a success of something different from his regular trade or profession. During his job-holding years, he should begin to cultivate at least in a small way what in his later or retired years he wishes to do. Ever so often people get into the news who are successful in a late vocation because they had done just that. For example, as a teen-ager in New Work, Ann Ives wanted to be an actress. But war and family obligations forced her into typing and Civil Service for thirty years. Yet all during those thirty years, writes Milton Lomask, she kept "working with amateur and semi-professional dramatic groups after hours. In other words, she kept a hand in" ("Afraid of Old Age," *Sign*, Apr., 1956). Upon her compulsory retirement, returning to New York, she took small television and summer theater jobs for three years, until in 1952 she was acclaimed as the *mother* in the stage hit, *Point of No Return*. Hers was the proper strategy for anyone who during the breadwinning days longs for laurels in some other field.

Among many other such examples we cite only a few. A rancher, Charles J. Belden of Pickford, Wyoming, liked to photograph people and places — and did. On retirement he made photography his profession and began selling to national magazines (see Doran K. Antrim, "Start Again at 65," *Catholic Digest*, July, 1957). A life insurance manager in Quebec, Jean Valenti, kept doing some hunting and fishing on the side. Upon retiring, he built a sportsman's lodge north of Montreal, and now operates it successfully for like-minded sportsmen. A Chicago school teacher, Mrs. George Furzer, upon retiring at 65, moved to Maryland. There, reports Milton Lomask, she "began doing full time what all her working days she had done spare-time — making fresh grated coconut and angel food cakes. By 1956 she was selling more than 2000 cakes and 2500 pies a month, baked in a new building by five bakers. She named them "Della's Cakes," for her daughter (*Sign*, Apr., 1956).

The most publicized example of success in a profession begun late is that of Thomas B. Costain, 73, whose novels like *The Black Rose, The Silver Chalice*, have sold in the millions. He was 57 years old before his first book was published. Since that late start he has written eight historical novels, three histories, one biography in collaboration. He has averaged a little less than a million copies on each, with a high of 2.7 million on the *Silver Chalice*.

When we analyze this sensational literary success of the later years, we discover first of all that Costain had since his school days been "intrigued by the historical novels of Alexandre Dumas and Sir Walter Scott." He himself explains significantly:

> For years I wanted to try this kind of writing, but I had my family to bring up. So I became an editor. I was with the Saturday Evening Post for fourteen years, then with Twentieth Century-Fox. Finally, when I was 55, I knew if I was ever going to write, I'd better start right away (see *Newsweek*, Sept. 23, 1957).

In other words, he had kept his hand in, so to speak, all his life for what in the later years he brilliantly started doing.

Doing on the side during one's professional years what one would like to do vocationally if circumstances permitted is the best advice for all of us. It is the best guarantee against frustration and boredom in retirement. Miss Olie A. Randall, Consultant, Community Service Society of New York, says pertinently:

> Old age is merely a stage of life in the sense that childhood and adolescence are stages. Just as a child should be prepared for adulthood, so a mature adult should prepare himself for the later maturity we call old age. You can start doing so at any point, at thirty or at sixty, but since the later years are the harvest years, it stands to reason that the sooner you start sowing, the more you'll reap when you reach them (Quoted from *Sign*, Apr., 1956, p. 55).

In short, the time to start any long-term project is now, the sooner the better. Unfortunately, at 65 it helps little to be told that the time to have started was at 35! Therefore, it is consoling to know that history provides many examples of persons who did start something new very late in life and did very well. It is good to find, that while it is wise to start early, it is seldom too late to start at all. Among celebrated examples which

history relates are that Cato began studying Greek at 80; Michelangelo, famed painter and architect, began to write poetry at 60;
Franklin started to study philosophy at 50, and Webster to study
seventeen different languages after fifty; Plutarch took his first
lesson in Latin at 80, and Socrates began playing musical instru-
ments at about 80; James Watt, inventor, learned German at 85;
and one Tom Scott is credited with starting Hebrew at 86;
Mary Baker Eddy established *The Christian Science Monitor*
when she was 87.

There are also noted instances more nearly in our time. Clara
Barton of Red Cross fame, who founded the American National
Association for First Aid when she was 84, learned to type at
89! Dr. Lillien Martin, who late in life founded the Old Age
Counseling Center in San Francisco, started to learn typing at 65
and to drive a car at 76! Everybody has read of Grandma Moses
— Mrs. Anna Mary Robertson Moses — who started painting at
79. When for her 98th birthday on September 7, 1958, she was
given "a red quilted robe" by another late-starter, Leo Schutzman,
now 80, "who took up painting when he was 73," it made the
news (*Newsweek*, Sept. 22, 1958). When James Wilson, an ex-
slave, described as the "Oldest Man in the U. S." died in
December, 1941, at the age of 120, his obituary notice said he
had been ordained a minister at 100:

> He worked as a farm hand until he was 100 years old, was
> ordained a Baptist minister after having attained that age, and
> added the serving of various Negro Baptist churches as pastor to
> his field of work until he was 117 years old (*New York Times*,
> Dec. 25, 1958).

Another news item (*Denver Register*, Aug. 17, 1958), pictures
an Indian seminarian in New Mexico "instructing his pagan 104-
year-old great-grandmother, Na glis des Bah, in the Catholic religion." Surely there is proof, that right up to the last breath it is
not too late to begin to learn!

Once the Associated Press carried a playful item entitled, "'How
to Live Long and Like It' Told in News: From 60 to Past 100
Is Time for Venturous" (Nov. 25, 1940). It listed among the

venturous a Pottsville, Pennsylvania, man who at 60 had just got his airplane pilot's license; a 73-year-old Gainsville, Florida, man as having just entered law school as a freshman; an 81-year-old Chester, South Carolina, woman as beginning a college course in astronomy; an 81-year-old San Diego man as having made his first solo flight in an airplane; a 73-year-old Burlington, Vermont, woman as having begun to ski; and a 75-year-old Claremont, California, man as having started his first novel. These individuals acting on the principle that it is seldom too late to start were, one can be sure, happier for their spirit of enterprise, regardless of the level of success they attained.

But especially inspiring for us and the world are the examples of late and successful vocations to the religious life. Years ago, in Milwaukee, I recall the excitement when a high school principal in his fifties, unmarried, resigned and entered a seminary, an oldster in a class of youths. With the false perspective of age peculiar to youth, his aspiration seemed to his young fellow students, while indeed noble, yet sadly futile — too late to succeed. But the gray-haired seminarian was in due time ordained and for a dozen or more years was a notably wise and able priest. But even while still a seminarian he proved to be a fatherly source of moderation and inspiration to his youthful fellow students. Had God called him from life before his ordination, his Tennysonian effort "to seek a newer world," the priesthood, so late in life would have been abundantly worthwhile — to himself certainly, but also for those who were near enough to feel the grace of his noble effort.

In the last year, several stories were carried in the news of men who happily had not thought it too late to start on a high vocation in their later years. Dr. Alfred O'Rahilly, once imprisoned for his fight for Irish Independence, long president of University College, Cork, author of books on money, electromagnetics, religion — practically a universal genius — started studying for the priesthood in his late sixties and was ordained in 1955 at the age of seventy. He went on to write a book entitled, *Gospel Meditations*, which Msgr. John S. Kennedy reviewed as gleaming with originality and "charged with vitality" (*Our Sunday Visitor*, Jan. 4, 1959). After so active a life, what could be more fitting and inspiring than to spend the later years of it as a priest of God, preparing himself to meet his Maker by being a shepherd to God's other sheep!

Similarly, a French ex-industrialist, Andre Lepoutre, was on July 5, 1958, ordained to the priesthood at 68. After his wife's death ten years ago, though he had five children and 25 grandchildren, he left his mills to his relatives and studied for the priesthood in the Benedictine Abbey of St. Andre near Bruges. Shortly after his ordination he had the satisfaction of officiating at the wedding of one of his granddaughters (see *Catholic Standard and Times*, July 18, 1958). How wonderful that Father Andre Lepoutre did not consider the sixties too late for aspiring to the holy priesthood, thus not only assuring almost certainly his own salvation, but also promoting that of his townsmen and relatives.

In the same month, another dispatch told about a Father Umberto Livieri, who became a priest at the age of 74. Father Umberto Livieri, O.S.B., had immigrated from Italy in 1921, worked fourteen years in the Bank of America, and for thirty years was professor of languages at Santa Clara University. In 1950 he began a lay apostolate "to spread the Gospel of Christ in sparsely settled sections of Mexico," where his "outstanding catechetical work" came to the attention of the Archbishop of Mexico. After the death of his wife he joined the Benedictines at the famous Subiaco Monastery in Italy to study for the priesthood. When the great day arrived, eight brothers and sisters proudly attended his ordination. Surely everyone would agree that here was a widower who made good — in the most blessed way.

These men who did not think the sixties and seventies too late to try for the new and exalted priestly vocation employed their later years in the wisest possible way. They had the satisfaction of doing something extraordinarily useful and important and they made their golden years a direct preparation for the golden gates of Paradise. But their example can be followed on other levels, religious and secular. Recently someone wrote that during a discussion of retirement he "was much impressed by the number of people retired and about to retire who expressed interest in finding employment in hospitals, missions, and such, where they might give their services without charge." He continued:

> I also expect to retire and, with my wife, would like to work for a year or more in a Catholic hospital, sanitarium, orphanage or mission in some area where the priests and nuns are hard pressed for funds and workers, such as in the South or Southwest. We would be self-supporting . . . (Brooklyn *Tablet*, Aug. 30, 1958).

Such a new start upon retirement as a lay missioner would be the best insurance for contentment and blessedness in the later years.

When our prime-of-life trade or profession becomes unpractical for us in the later years, we should not dismiss as too late the hope of developing a new vocation or avocation. Whether it be an exalted or modest one, as long as it is good for mankind, it will make for a happy and creative old age. One widow in her seventies said of her new environment, "I was lonely when I first moved here." She complained that she had been considered too old to mow her own lawn or wash her windows. Then she started taking gym and swimming lessons at the local YMCA, became a senior citizen swimming "champ," and now, at 80, finds great joy teaching children calisthenics (Phila. *Inquirer*, Dec. 28, 1958). Another headline reads: "Never Too Old to Go to Work" (Philadelphia *Daily News*, Jan. 2, 1959). It tells the story of a well-to-do, married woman, who, in her seventies, tired of the social life, reflected, "I just thought it would be rather fun to be employed in business." So at 74, with some smooth talking, she got herself enrolled in the Chase School of New York for training as a telephone switchboard operator. She finished her course, and the Director of the school, Mrs. Chase, reports, "She was an immediate hit. She is one of the most energetic phone operators in town."

These instances illustrate that while it is better to start early, the most important thing is to start — even if late. Most of us during our young and middle years, when our material and spiritual investments should be made, too often and too easily forget the urgency of time. We delay and postpone things, often our innermost aspiration and ambitions, as if the future stretched long and leisurely before us.

But the future that looks so distant and timeless at twenty, runs on toward sixty, if not always smoothly, yet always swiftly and inexorably. Like a thief in the night, retirement will seem to have been lurking just around the corner — with so many hopes unfulfilled, with so much still to do — things other than just making a living — and only the later years to do them. When, with perhaps a shock, we realize that the later years are indeed upon us, then it is especially urgent to remind ourselves that these are both the last and the golden opportunity of our life. They are the time to exclaim with Tennyson's Ulysses, " 'Tis not too late to seek a newer world. . . . Old age hath yet his honor and his toil. / Death closes all; but something ere the end, / Some work of noble note, may yet be done. . . ." And then start doing it — practically and resolutely, for contentment here, and heaven hereafter.

CHAPTER III

Man's Maximum Earthly Life Span

THE spur that jogs us mortals to make the most of our years is the reflection that like the sand in the hourglass our years will run out. Some years ago, Dr. Robert W. McKenna in *The Adventure of Death* (Putnam, 1917), wrote,

> Practically all the progress that man has made is due to the fact that he is mortal. If man knew that his days on earth were to be endless, all incentive to bestir himself — except to seek food and clothing — would be lost. There would be . . . no hungry aspiration to be remembered after he is dead. If there were no death, life would become a thing stagnant, monotonous and unspeakably burdensome.

Nevertheless, ever since God drove the first parents from Paradise and condemned them to die for their disobedience, man — ancient and modern — has kept up furtive hope and wishful search for an eternal earthly life. Appropriately, Florida, where people now go to live longer, was according to legend first explored by Ponce de Leon because it was rumored to have a fountain of eternal youth. That hope, especially in materialistic minds, never completely dies.

The dramatic rise everywhere of the average life expectancy in the past half century — from 49 years in 1900 to 70.2 years in 1958 in the United States — has given rise to speculations as to the possibility of an unlimited prolongation of the life span. Coupled with medicine's victory over several once devastating plagues, the rising life span has caused a few materialists to hope that perhaps someday man can, like unto the gods, live forever

22

on this earth. Such earthly immortality is subconsciously equated with the earthly paradise which Adam knew!

Others more modestly have searched in the Bible for confirmation that the life span may indeed be extended considerably above what it is now. The Psalmist's declaration that our years "are three score and ten" has in the Christian world already virtually become a fact. When he elaborates, "But if in the strong they be fourscore years, and what is more of them is labor and sorrow" (Ps. 89), he is being thought unwarrantedly pessimistic by many geriatricians. These point to some million and a half Americans 80 and over most of whom seem to have little sorrow and still less labor! More and more geriatricians, when they quote Ecclesiasticus, "The number of the days of man at the most are a hundred" (18:8), prefer to consider that a future average rather than a maximum. They quote Genesis with approval as a literal possibility and goal, "And God said . . . [man's] days shall be a hundred and twenty years" (6:3).

On the other hand, they do regard with a good deal of skepticism the publicized instances of Methuselahs in the past. Of the latter's reputed 969 years, a Yale scholar, Dr. Andrew Efron, suggested that a proper interpretation of the Old Testament would bring that number down to 192 (*New York Times Magazine*, Sept. 8, 1940). Rationalist scholars tend to discount the longevity of the Patriarchs; Catholic exegetes in a similar vein explain, as the *Catholic Encyclopedia* puts it, "that the year meant by the sacred writer is not the equivalent of our year." Secular instances of extreme longevity regarded skeptically by gerontologists include the following: Petratsch Zorten, a Hungarian cowherd, supposed to have lived to 185 on a diet of milk, cake, and brandy; Henry Jenkins, a Yorkshire laborer, 169; Thomas Parr, Shropshire, England, 152; and Christian Jacobsen Drakenberg, between 141 and 146. This Dane is said to have been enslaved by the Algerians at 68, escaped at 83, joined the Danish navy at 84, married at 111, became a widower at 130, proposed to numerous women until he was 140. At this age he gave up proposing and led "quite a respectable life" until his death in

1772 at 146 — which, however, some sources reduced to 141!

To these historical cases of incredible longevity, our own time adds names. In April, 1958, the Columbian, Javier Pereira, died at a reputed 168. In 1956, this toothless Indian 4 feet 3 inches short, weighing only 75 pounds, was examined for nine days at the Cornell Medical Center in New York. After the doctors had made hundreds of X rays and tapped his veins, they reported, "Mr. Pereira is indeed a very old man, . . . possibly may be more than 150 years of age." His formula for longevity was, "Don't worry, drink a lot of coffee, and smoke a good cigar" (*Newsweek*, Apr. 14, 1958). A Russian Azerbaijan farmer, Mawhmud Fivazov, was pictured as celebrating his 150th birthday. According to *Newsweek* (June 30, 1958), "Sire of 23 sons and daughters, Fivazov's family now consist of 152 persons, of whom the eldest, a daughter, is now about 122. A government doctor keeps check on his health, but so far has revealed no 'secret' of longevity." According to the picture, this man looks like a hale and hearty fellow of about 75.

Two cases were reported in an AP dispatch of Dec., 1958, from Iran. There a peasant, Reza Shirsavar of the Mazanderan District, was said to be 145, and still active as a detective! Another native of the village of Kelusah claimed to be 185. After two doctors examined him, they issued this communique: "In the course of the examination the age of Sayed Ali Saleh Kutahi was estimated between 158 and 188."

What is disconcerting about these sensational cases of "Methuselitis" is that they seem only to occur in faraway, rather primitive countries where those reputedly so long on years are provokingly short on birth certificates. Gerontologists are skeptical. They suspect that some of these cases may really be father-son combinations. Dr. Nathan W. Shock, Chief, Section on Gerontology, U. S. Public Health Service, when, at a Convention of the Gerontological Society, in Philadelphia, in November 1958, I called to his attention a Peruvian reputedly 150 brought to New York for study, expressed doubt of such fantastic ages and said: I want to see the birth certificates."

In this country, the best we seem to come up with is centenarians adding another decade or so. In 1956, the last veteran of the Union Army, Albert Woolson, died at 109. On March 16, 1958, John Sallings, of Kingsport, Tennessee, died of pneumonia at 112. He had been one of the two last survivors of the Confederate Army. At his death, the lone survivor was Walter Williams, described then as "a frail, bedridden man of 116 who lives in Houston, Texas" (*New York Herald Tribune*, Mar. 17, 1958). Mr. Williams also died in December, 1959. When in December, 1945, the ex-slave, "Uncle" Jim Wilson, who at a hundred had been ordained a Baptist minister, died at a reputed 120, he was described as "the oldest citizen in the United States . . . his official census record showing May 15, 1825, as his birth date" (*New York Times*, Dec. 25, 1945). Apparently there was no birth certificate!

So far, 120 seems to be about the recognized upper limit of man's life span. The National Geographic Society in an AP dispatch (Apr. 12, 1954) reported rather positively "that most experts agree that 112, 113, or maybe even 115 appears to be a maximum length of human life." That does seem to be the prevailing view of the gerontologists. Dr. Edward J. Stieglitz, regarded as an "Expert on Factors That Influence Length and Fullness of Life," said in a *U. S. News* interview (Feb. 14, 1958): "Probably the normal life span of man is between 100 and 120, at the most."

Though a top longevity of 120 years is the most accepted view, some are less conservative. Prof. R. W. Gerard, University of Chicago physiologist, is reported as holding that "man's true life span is almost twice the biblical three score and ten." The Russian professor, Alexander A. Bogomolets uses the formula of the French naturalist Buffon, according to which any organism normally has a life span six times that of its period of growth. Accordingly Bogomolets calculates that man's "normal life span should be from 120 to 150 years." He has announced a serum which, by regenerating the connective tissue cells of the body, should prolong life ("Tomorrow You May Be Younger," *Reader's*

LIBRARY
College of St. Francis
JOLIET, ILL.

112,342

Digest, Feb., 1946). Dr. Shock, referring to "Bogomolets' antireticular cytotoxic serum, a kind of witch's broth," doubts its effectiveness in prolonging life. In fact, little has been said of it after its first publicizing.[1]

Just as so far no medicinal elixir of youth has been discovered, so the centenarians have not been able to reveal the secret of their long life. Their recipes tend to be contradictory and of little help. One Philadelphia centenarian attributed his long life to eating hasty pudding; a woman, 101, of Reading, Pennsylvania, said, "Late to bed and late to rise / Keeps the twinkle in my eyes." An elderly French doctor, still only in the eighties and obviously unlikely to reach 100, said, "Don't drink any water and take as little exercise as possible!" More authentically Dr. John B. Cummins, Fort Worth, Texas, the nation's oldest practicing physician, said on his hundredth birthday, "I'm regular in my habits. No alcohol. No tobacco. Never exceed my limits. I eat regular — anything the restaurants hand out. But, I don't take big quantities. I only weigh 100 pounds, and I'm 5 feet 11 inches tall" (*Newsweek*, Dec. 1, 1958). At a hundred he is still physically and mentally spry; he is reported as reading without glasses, having good hearing, possessed of all but two of his original teeth. He is not only practicing general medicine but performing, for example, Caesarean operations.

Under such conditions, the Psalmist's gloomy note that what is more than fourscore is "labor and sorrow" would seem to be false. What is really the secret that makes for nonagenarians and centenarians? So far at least science does not know it, nor can doctors guarantee long life whether to themselves or to others.

---

[1] See *U. S. News*, Oct. 23, 1953, p. 88.

The following comparative figures between the life span of man and that of other living things may be of interest. An item in the New York *Times Magazine* (Sept. 8, 1940) gives these figures: "Man is about the longest-lived of the mammals, with the elephant running a close second. For other types of life Dr. Raymond Pearl of Johns Hopkins sets these maximums: insects, 17 years; fish, 267 years; reptiles, 175 years; birds, 118 years. These spans are dwarfed by trees — the giant California redwoods, whose annual growth rings reveal ages running to 5000 years, and the macrozamia trees, found in the Tambourine Mountains of Australia, one of which has been estimated to be 15,000 years old."

LIBRARY
College of St. Francis
JOLIET, ILL.

Dr. Logan Clendening, who fifteen years ago and more, was syndicating a daily "Diet and Health" column to 383 newspapers, once wrote:

> Most of the authors of works on longevity die young. The only exception was an Italian, Luigi Carnero; he advised a system of living to promote longevity and he lived to be ninety himself. But he was over seventy-five when he began to advise on how to live long (*Scranton Times*, Oct. 14, 1941).

Dr. Clendening himself held that "One hundred years is the upper limit of the span of human life," that "if you are aiming at longevity, you should begin with your grandparents," and that "except in extreme cases of lack of moderation, it makes very little difference what you do after fifty." He thought it best to determine one's diet by that "very efficient monitor — the appetite," and once declared that "what the country needed was a good five cent shot of whisky." Unfortunately, at sixty Dr. Clendening, believing that his own health was getting bad, committed suicide. During the same week, another doctor, whom *Time* described as "a second mass-merchandiser of health advice," Dr. Irving S. Cutter died of cancer, at 69. He had been writing a column on "How to Keep Well" for fifty newspapers. When it comes to the old proverb, "Physician, heal thyself," most doctors readily admit that, while they know why people die young, they do not know what keeps some few alive into the high eighties and nineties.

At present, though the average life expectancy at birth has jumped dramatically from about fifty in 1900 to seventy in 1960, gerontologists point out that this is not so much because older people get much older than formerly but because fewer people die young. Medical science, having concentrated successfully on the ailments of the first forty years, such as smallpox, diphtheria, tuberculosis, typhoid fever, now helps millions into the second forty years who formerly succumbed in the first. For youths under twenty, average life expectancy has increased some twenty years since 1900, but for people over sixty the increase has been only some three years. In 1900, a person of sixty had a further life expectancy of 14.7 years; but in 1955 the sixty-year-old could expect to live 17.5 years, which is only 2.8 years more. In 1900 someone seventy had an expectancy of 9.3 more years; in 1955, one of 11.3. Still more significant, the person who reached eighty in 1900 could expect to live 5.2 years more, whereas in 1955 he could expect 6.6 years more. In other words, once someone in 1900 safely reached the later years, he could expect to live almost as long as anyone who reaches eighty now — only one to three fewer years.

Some authorities consider this relatively small rise of longevity in the decades after sixty as a signal that the biblical four score years does represent the top expectancy. Corson and McConnell write:

> Opinions differ on the likelihood of much reduction in death rates. Skeptics cite the decline in the death rate from 17.2 per 1,000 in 1900 to 10.1 in 1947 and an estimated 9.6 in 1953 and contend that further significant reductions are unlikely.[2]

However, all gerontologists expect at least some further lengthening of the average life span, including that of those already in the later years. They contend that medical science has only begun its campaign against the typical diseases of the aged. They point out that the introduction of serum treatments, of sulfa drugs, of penicillin has already caused a notable drop in the death rate of the aged. A sensible forecast seems to be that medical science can increase the average life expectancy of the aged another ten years or so. Dr. Shock writes:

> The probable effects of eliminating the primary causes of death among the aged (diseases of the heart, blood vessels, and kidneys, and cancer) have been calculated as adding approximately 10 years to life expectancy. Thus, at age 70, current life expectancy of approximately 10 years would be increased to 20 years.[3]

In other words, anyone who has successfully breasted the sea of

[2] John J. Corson and John W. McConnell, *Economic Needs of Older People*, The Twentieth Century Fund, New York, 1956, p. 12.

[3] Nathan W. Shock, *Trends in Gerontology*, 2nd ed. (Stanford, Calif.: Stanford University Press, 1957), p. 14.

life as far as seventy will, after medical science has achieved its
full beneficence, have an average chance of living to ninety.

One puzzling, as well as encouraging, factor is that people do
not seem to die of old age but of some disease. Dr. Edward L.
Bortz, Chief of Medical Services, Lankenau Hospital, Philadelphia, writes:

> . . . there is no verified report of anyone dying of old age.
> The most common diseases of longevity are blood vessel break-
> down, cancer, rheumatism and mental deterioration. But none of
> these is inevitable; and now there is exciting evidence that many
> patients with these conditions can be cured . . . evidence is now
> at hand that the period of healthy existence can be prolonged.[4]

Dr. Shock holds that if the diseases peculiar to old age can be
checked we do not know how long people might live (Interview,
Nov. 7, 1958). But Dr. Ernst Boas in *Add Life to Your Years*
([New York: McBride, 1954], p. 5) assumes that "even under
ideal circumstances and with avoidance of all of the diseases which
may shorten life years, the maximum life span will hardly exceed
a hundred years. . . ." He regards this "as the innate constitu-
tionally determined life span of the human race." This theory
echoes somewhat the philosophy of "The Deacon's Masterpiece,"
the poem about "the Wonderful 'One-Hoss-Shay'" by Oliver
Wendell Holmes, also a physician. In this shay the deacon had
made every part perfect. Since no part could give way, he figured
it to last forever. Nevertheless, a hundred years later, though it
revealed only "A general flavor of mild decay, but nothing local,"
the poor old buggy "went to pieces all at once . . . and nothing
first"! Somewhat from a similar viewpoint, Professor Drake writes:

> Basically there seems to be one reason that death rates for
> the aged cannot be reduced much further. This reason is that
> people are going to die sooner or later and if they are saved
> from death by one disease they will die from some other disease.[5]

[4] *Aging Is Everyone's Concern*, The Proceedings of the First Ontario
Conference on Aging, 1957, University of Toronto, p. 5.

[5] Joseph T. Drake, Professor of Sociology, Davidson College, *The Aged in
American Society* (New York: The Ronald Press, 1958), p. 53.

We leave the matter of man's maximum earthly life span, as science now estimates it for the future, with the optimistic statement of the Proceedings of the First Ontario Conference on Aging, 1957:

> Data now points to an increase in the span of life for the experimental animals as much as 30 per cent. A biological timetable for the human life span, as predicted by a number of authorities, suggests 100 to 125 years as average (*Aging is Everyone's Concern*, p. 5.).

CHAPTER IV

The Average Life Span in Our Time

WHETHER the life span in the future will go up to 100 or even to 125 is, of course, still only speculation — and in any case its doing so would no longer help us. But what is pertinent for us is that even now the average life expectancy is much higher than it was for our great-grandparents. In fact, it is hovering slightly above the "three score and ten" given as the optimum by Psalm 89. In this country, about one and a quarter million become 65 every year. In 1959 about 15,000,000 were 65 and over; in 1975, according to projections, there will be 20,000,000.

Loneliness has often been thought the affliction of old age. In our time however, it should not be for want of companions our age. Not even if we reach the Psalmist's fourscore years of "the strong," for in 1957, there were 2,239,000 men and women eighty and over.[1] When Oliver Wendell Holmes in "The Last Leaf" immortalized the lone survivor of the Boston Tea Party of 1773,

---

[1] *Current Population Reports*, Bureau of the Census, Dec. 18, 1957, p. 16. Of these 2,239,000, 608,000 men and 798,000 women were between 80 and 84; 348,000 men and 485,000 women were 85 and over.

Populations statistics are tricky in that as soon as a figure is set down, someone dies or is born. Yet sometimes, if available, a precise figure is preferable to a round number. I give one or the other as expedient, but preferably the exact one, in spite of the dangers. While it is not expedient to give the source or reference for every figure used in the book, each is well authenticated. The regular sources for them are the Bureau of Census Reports, especially that for December 18, 1957, for November 10, 1958, and for March 19, 1958. Another often used source is the United Nations Population Study No. 26, *The Aging of Populations and Its Economic and Social Implications*, New York, 1956. Still another is the *Statistical Bulletin*, Metropolitan Life Insurance Co., New York, of Nov., 1957, Mar., 1958, Apr., 1958, and June, 1958.

this old gentleman, whose friends had all passed away, was in his eighties. Holmes represents him as tottering along the streets, forlorn, shaking his feeble head as if to say, "they are gone, . . . the names he loved to hear / Have been carved for many a year / On the tomb."

In 1830 anyone reaching eighty was rare and exceptional. Though official statistics are wanting, one can calculate the total for the country as fewer than 45,000. Twenty years later, in 1850, when the population had almost doubled to 23,191,876, there were only 77,383 octogenarians, 11,695 nonagenarians and, surprisingly, 2555 centenarians. Halving these figures for 1830, we find that Holmes's old veteran would have found only one man or woman his age or older in every forty square miles on the average.[2]

Now, however, a veteran of eighty would hardly be "the last leaf" in any community. In 1957 he would have had 2,239,000 companions his age or older. A staggering total of 14,749,000 were 65 or over, and of these 1,406,000 were between 80 and 84, 833,000 were 85 or more, and almost 5000 were 100 or more! Ecclesiasticus wrote, "He that honoreth his father shall enjoy a long life" (3:7). The large number of men eighty and more in our time, 1,036,000 projected for 1960, would suggest that these gentlemen when young must have held their fathers in great honor! But the number of women eighty and over, 1,448,000, heavily exceeds the men. Ecclesiasticus also declared, "Happy is the husband of a good wife: for the number of his years is double" (26:1)! Since the Census projects 6,983,000 men between 65 and 79 in 1960, 675,000 between 80 and 84, and 361,000 of 85 and over, one reflects with edification that they must have marvelously good wives to be enjoying this doubling of their years.

Furthermore, even if there were no available statistics, one could assume as a foregone conclusion that the Lord, who according to the Psalmist will fill "with length of days" as well as sanc-

---

[2] In 1830, in a white population of 10,539,378, only 420,840 were sixty or over. In a Negro population of 2,328,642, no figures for 65 are available but those 55 or over numbered 25,589 free and 84,405 slave.

tifying grace anyone who "dwelleth in the aid of the most High" (Ps. 90:16), would reward the good wives who "doubled" their husbands' years with an equally long life at least. Indeed, statistics do show incontestably that the Lord grants the ladies, as figured from birth, a life span averaging 6.4 years better than the men's. The Census projects 7,212,000 women between 65 and 79 for 1960, another 922,000 between 80 and 84, and 526,000 of 85 and over. Furthermore the ratio is widening steadily in favor of the women. In 1950 there were still ninety-five men 65 and over to 100 women; by 1957 there were only 85 to a 100; and by 1980 predicts the Bureau of the Census "there will be only 72 males per 100 females in the aged population, and an excess of 4 million women 65 and over."

Nevertheless, while the Lord is seeing fit to let the women in this country (and in all the old Christian countries) outlive the men by an increasing margin, He does give every man, as well as woman, who is old enough now to read this all the odds in favor of living well into the later years. At fifty, a white man has a life expectancy of another 23.1 years, a woman of 27.7 years.[3] If you are white, male, and temperate, and have reached 45, the odds are that you will live into the later years until 74.3; if you have already reached 65, the odds are you will reach 79.2. Your sister, however, if 45 has odds of reaching 77.1; if she is 65, odds of reaching 80.5. While at birth the life expectancy of the women is 6.4 years longer, at 65 it is only 1.3 years longer than that of men, but at all the stages the life expectancy of women exceeds that of men.

For both men and women the proportion reaching 65 has jumped sensationally since 1900. At that time only 4.1 per cent were 65 or over (3,080,498). Between 1900 and 1940, the population increased 75 per cent but the number of persons 65 and

---

[3] Figures from *Statistical Bulletin*, Metropolitan Life Insurance Co., June, 1938. Because of the marked difference in the life expectancy between white and nonwhite, statistics often have to be broken down. At fifty, a Negro's expectancy is another 21.1 years; a colored woman's is 24.1. At birth the life expectancy of white males is 67.3; of white females, 73.7; of nonwhite males, 61.1; of nonwhite females, 65.9.

over increased 300 per cent and constituted 6.9 per cent of the total (9,019,314). Again between 1940 and 1950, the proportion of people 65 and over reached 8.2 per cent (12,322,000). By 1957 it was 8.8 per cent (14,407,000). For 1960 the Census projects 15,779,000 persons 65 and over, and estimates that by 1980 "the group may number about 24½ million . . . a gain of roughly one-half million annually" (*Report*, Nov. 10, 1958, p. 4). We remind ourselves that we ourselves are components of these statistics!

In all countries, but most markedly in the mature Christian ones, life expectancy at birth has increased. In the advanced Christian countries the number and proportion of people 65 and over are increasing sensationally. The *Population Study No. 26* of the United Nations (New York, 1956) gives figures and percentages for twenty-six countries classified as either "developed" or "underdeveloped." Excepting Latin America, the developed countries are also the Christian countries. These have by far the longest life span and a strikingly large proportion of people 65 and older. In Togoland, Africa, for example, underdeveloped and non-Christian, only 1.46 per cent of the people are over 64, whereas in France, the center of Christendom, the percentage is a staggering 11.79 per cent. In the Gold Coast of Africa, only 1.52 per cent are oldsters; but in Belgium, 11.05 per cent. In Algeria, 2.70 per cent; in Britain, 10.83 per cent; in Burma, 2.83 per cent; in Ireland, not industrial but intensely Christian, 10.69 per cent; in Formosa, 2.50 per cent; in Sweden, 10.32 per cent. In Israel, rather industrial but not Christian, it is 4.00 per cent; in Austria, 10.13 per cent; in India, 3.38 per cent; in Switzerland, 9.57 per cent; in Turkey, 3.41 per cent; in West Germany, 9.28 per cent. In Soviet Russia, only 4.10 per cent of the people are 65 and over; but in Canada it is 7.75 per cent.

Japan is often regarded as the most advanced non-Christian country. Since Commodore C. Perry on July 14, 1853, introduced western commerce, it has made the most determined effort to learn from the Christian West. Its proportion of oldsters is 4.94 per cent; but that of the United States, even though it includes a large nonwhite population with a shorter life span, is 8.18 per cent.[4]

In general, the more Christian a country, the greater the proportion of people who live into the later years. Within a country, the groups with the longest tradition of Christian living have the best life expectancy: those with a Christian European background in America have a greater proportion of oldsters than those of a pagan, non-European background. Long life seems to be one of the fruits of Christian living. The percentage of oldsters in the Christian countries is almost twice that in the pagan countries, even in Japan.

But curiously, this is not true of the Latin-American countries, all of which are surpassed by Japan, including Peru with its 4.32 per cent of oldsters. Whereas even Spain, considered of similar race and not very industrial, has 7.23 per cent oldsters, Argentina the second highest has only 3.92. Whereas Portugal has 6.98 per cent, Brazil with the same language has only 2.45 per cent. Whereas Italy, also of the Latin race, has 8.06 per cent oldsters, Chili has only 3.50 per cent, Mexico, 3.36 per cent, and Panama, 3.23 per cent. Puerto Rico, though under American rule since 1898, has only 3.80 per cent oldsters, slightly under Peru and Argentina.

If one of the fruits of Christianity is longevity, as certainly seems to be indicated by the superior life span of the old-line Christian countries over that of the pagan and Moslem countries, then the disappointing life span of the Latin-American countries, nominally Catholic, should be explained. Of course, these nations

---

[4] In 1957, according to Bureau of Census figures (Dec. 18, 1957, No. 170), 9.1 per cent of whites in the United States were 65 or over, but only 5.3 per cent of the nonwhite population of 18,766,000. The percentage of 5.3 per cent nevertheless shows a better life expectancy of the American Negro than that of any of the non-Christian peoples of the world. Another interesting point is that the percentage of Negroes who reach 85 and more is about the same as for whites. In 1957, among 13,743,000 whites 64 and over, 1,314,000 or 9 per cent were between 80 and 84, and 750,000 or 5 per cent (4 per cent men, but 6 per cent women) were 85 or more. Among the 1,006,000 Negroes 65 and over, 92,000 or only 5 per cent were between 80 and 84, but 83,000 men and women were 85 and over, which is 4 per cent, equaling the percentage of white men 85 and over.

are not industrial, but neither is vigorously Christian Ireland, in which a high 10.69 per cent are in the later years. The explanation seems to be that although Latin America has for a few hundred years been nominally Catholic, the vast majority of natives, really Indians and Mestizos, have been little more than scratched by Christianity. Just as the United States, despite its commendable and costly efforts and programs, has not in half a century been able to convert its two million Puerto Ricans to the more civilized ways that make for longevity, so Catholicism with its meager resources has not in four hundred years been able to transform the cannibalistic natives of 1530 into clean-living, hygienic Christian human beings, whose corollary reward for their Christian living is a long average life span.

The life span quite certainly increases on the average not only with the advance in medical and social sciences but also with the practice of certain customs, habits, and virtues. Christianity, though aimed at souls, also stimulates such natural virtues and customs as make for better bodies to house these souls. Whatever makes for goodness will also make for longevity. Even on an individual basis, the good tend to live long and the few who do not, like Teresa of Lisieux, are the proverbial exceptions. Their demise is usually due to special conditions — heredity, contagion, accident. If the good generally died young, there would be notoriety in the circumstance that most of the popes got into their full stride at 65, when the average world retires!

In a novel about the old monastery, Maria-Morgenstern, in the German Black Forest, Thomas Kernan, who had been interned in its vicinity, commented in his novel (*Now With the Morning Star*) that "once past the novitiate few monks ever went away," and that "They lived to fantastic old ages. To die at seventy was to die young." In a study on the *Longevity of Members of Catholic Religious Sisterhoods* (Dissertation, Catholic University, 1927), Dr. C. J. Fecher incidentally cites an authority to the effect that in New York City clergymen, along with school teachers, have "the most favorable mortality in a list of representative occupations" (p. 48), and found that sisters in every period of life have a lower death rate than women of the general population, married and unmarried (p. 53). His latest findings "with respect to mortality and longevity of 90,000 sisters in 90 communities" from 1900 to 1954 indicate "that the Sisters enjoy three additional years at age 20 as compared to white females (married and single) in the general population" (Letter, July 7, 1959).

Cardinal A. J. Muench, while bishop of Fargo, North Dakota, urging Lenten fasting wrote:

> It is striking to note that hermits who lived on a very plain diet reached five score and more — St. Romuald, founder of the Camaldolese monks, reached the age of 120 years, St. Paul the First Hermit attained the age of 113, and St. Anthony the Hermit, who fasted to such an extent that he added nothing but salt to his bread, and quenched his thirst with water, lived to see 105 years. Longevity is a characteristic of all orders whose members fast much and eat little meat if any, such as Cistercians, Carthusians, Camaldolese, Trappists, and other similar monastic orders (*Catholic Action News*, Fargo, N. Dak., Mar., 1958).

These monastic centenarians here cited for their fasting were not simply good, they were extraordinarily good and saintly, and they broke all the life expectancy tables! As an idea, I jotted down fifteen literary saints just as they came to my mind and then checked their ages. The average, even though it included St. Francis of Assisi, afflicted with stigmata, who died at 45, and St. Thomas Aquinas, abnormally corpulent, who died at 49, proved to be 64.8, virtually 65.[5] When we reflect that these saints lived in times and climes when the average life expectancy ranged between a low of twenty-two years in the Roman Empire and a high in Western Europe before 1850 of perhaps forty, their

---

[5] The names in alphabetical order with dates as usually stated and ages, are as follows: Anselm (1030–1109), 66; Athanasius (295–373), 78; Augustine, not as sinful as he sounds in his *Confessions*, (354–430), 76; Bede (673–735), 62; Benedict (480–547), 67; Bernard (1090–1153), 63; Bonaventure (1221–1274), 53; Boniface, martyred, date of birth disputed (675–755), 80; Bridget (1303–1373), 70; Francis of Assisi (1181–1226), 45; Francis de Sales (1567–1622), 55; Ignatius (1491–1556), 65; Isadore (560–636), 76; Theresa of Avila (1515–1582), 67; and Thomas Aquinas (1225–1274), 49.

average longevity of 65 is remarkable. It is accentuated by the fact that nearly all of them were much harassed and over-worked, too.

A cursory glance at a few typical English and American writers tends to confirm the observation that the good (the moderate and temperate) live long, the intemperate and reckless die young. Popularly one thinks of Byron, Shelley, Poe as rather "fast" fellows; and Tennyson, Longfellow, Wordsworth as rather good and moralistic. Byron died at 36, Poe at 40, Shelley at 30 (lost at sea, not without suspicion of suicide). Tennyson, on the other hand died at 83, Longfellow at 75, Wordsworth at 80. Among the playrights one thinks of Greene, Goldsmith, Synge, and Wilde as less than models of sobriety. Greene, notorious for calling Shakespeare "an upstart crow," died miserably at 32,[6] Goldsmith at 46, Synge at 38, and Wilde at 44. One thinks of Ben Jonson, Barrie, Shaw, Maxwell Anderson as rather proper. Jonson died at 64, Barrie at 77, Shaw at 94, and Anderson is still writing at 71. With but a few exceptions one could go on indefinitely enumerating cases showing that sobriety and propriety pay off in longer life and the converse carry the penalty of shortened years.

Indeed it should be obvious that the best Christian morals tend to produce the longest life. Conversely, sin and vice lead to premature decline. Dr. Charles P. Bruehl in *This Way Happiness* (Bruce, 1941) wrote that morality conforms to human nature and is for the general good of man, including the biological requirements of his existence:

> Mental and physical health are fostered by obedience to the moral laws and nothing favors mental breakdown and physical disintegration more than certain vices (p. 113).

---

[6] On his premature deathbed, the profligate Greene, in *A Groatsworth of Wit Bought With a Million of Repentance*, warned his friends: "Remember, gentlemen, your lives are like so many lighted tapers, that are with care delivered to all of you to maintain: these with wind-puffed wrath may be extinguished, with drunkenness put out, with negligence let fall; for man's time is not of itself so short but it is more shortened by sin. The fire of my life is now at the last snuff."

But lest someone pose the case of Benjamin Franklin, who reached 84, and Goethe, who reached 83, both in full mental vigor, yet both having left proofs of grave sins against the Sixth Commandment, we must explain that what shortens life is not the sin of it but the excess and intemperance of it. What tends to prolong life is not the lack of sin as such, but the moderation and temperateness that characterize morality. Franklin and Goethe, even when sinful, were consciously and exceptionally moderate and controlled. Nature punishes the excess, not the sin. Conceivably, excessive ardor in marriage could debilitate more seriously than extramarital sin so spaced and regulated as Franklin prescribed for himself. He and Goethe — and others that could be named in this connection — were endowed with uncommon strength of will and worldly prudence enabling them to time and control their sins so as not to harm their bodies. For most human beings, however, any willful indulgence in sin as a way of life weakens their will and their prudence. It corrodes their common sense. They tend to slump more and more into vice and recklessness — until not only their soul is mortally wounded but their body, too.

Much of the modern increase in longevity is due merely to the natural virtues — to hygiene, diet, temperance, and sex control (at least to the point of avoidance of promiscuity and prostitution). These natural virtues, which give to the people of the Western nations a strikingly longer life span, should not be ignored or undervalued. They seem to be a product or a corollary of Christianity. They continue their beneficence in countries whose culture is Christian, even after, as in France and perhaps also America, much of the conscious or theological Christian impetus has become submerged.

At any rate, the life span in culturally Christian and relatively sober-living America and Europe has increased enormously in the past hundred years. The *United Nations* Study No. 26 found that in the developed countries (which happen to equate with Christian) "mortality rates at all ages have considerably declined

during the last hundred years" (Dec., 1956). In 1945, the old
Colliers Magazine said correctly:

> Americans had a life expectancy at birth of 35 years in 1800,
> of 39 years in 1850, of 49 years in 1900; while today it is 65 years.

Eleven years later, in 1956, it had risen to 69.2; in 1958, to 70.2.

According to the U.N. Study No. 26, the mere rise in the
number of older people has "stimulated interest in the social and
medical care of the aged" so that this "increasing concern with
the well-being of the aged may contribute to the lengthening
of many lives."

What concerns you and me is that, if we take reasonable care
of ourselves and have normal luck, we can all expect to get old
and to be in the later years for a long time. If we are forty, we
can on the average expect to live another 33.7 years; if fifty,
another 25.1; if sixty, another 17.5; and if seventy, another 11
years. If we happen to be the optimistic sort we can hope to do
better than the average. And if we are men, we can be fairly
certain that most of our beloved women folk will be around to
press the rosary into our hand during our last anxious hour —
for at birth the life expectancy of white women is 73.7 as against
67.3 for the men. After reaching 65, though our wives and sisters
will outlive us by 2.6 years for an average of 15.5, we men can
hope for another 12.9 years. Since this is generously more than
the "threescore and ten" allotted by the old Psalmist, we can
be more than content with our life span — provided we ourselves
make the average!

CHAPTER V

Reaching the Full Life Expectancy Ourselves

HOWEVER blissful heaven may be, most of us are not anxious to get there fast. Except possibly in the saints, our mortal nature prompts to want to live as long as possible. It has been said that no one is so old as not to expect to live at least another year. It is natural, therefore, when the actuaries tell us that the average life expectancy at 50 is another 25.1 years and at 60 another 17.5, we want to do what we can to reach the fullness of the average ourselves.

Unfortunately about the very first recipe for equaling or beating the life expectancy tables we are too late to apply! Virtually all the gerontologists agree that one of the surest ways to live long is to have had parents and grandparents who lived long. Most of them quote the poet and doctor Oliver Wendell Holmes, who said, "If you are setting out to achieve three score years and twenty, the first thing to be done is, some years before birth to advertise for a couple of parents both belonging to long-lived families." In the Second International Gerontological Congress in St. Louis, Dr. E. Jalavisto of Helsinki said that our chance of a long life depends more on whether the mother lived longer than the father. But most experts do not distinguish between the parents. Dr. Stieglitz in *The Second Forty Years* (New York: Lippincott, 1952, p. 43) said insurance underwriters are justified in considering family history. "Biologic inheritance," he found, "may affect longevity in two ways: the quality of the germ plasm conditions the rate of senescence and it also affects the indi-

41

vidual's vulnerability to disease." In short, some inherited genes make for both a longer and a healthier life.

Happily however for those of us who did not pick long-lived parents, the gerontologists merely say that if we did pick such parents we are very likely to reach and surpass the biblical four-score and ten. They do not affirm, however, that if we had parents who died young we too will necessarily die young. Dr. Shock, in an interview which *U.S. News* (Oct. 23, 1953) entitled, "Can You Stay Young Longer?" said that while "certainly heredity is an important factor in longevity . . . I prefer to assume a 50-50 distribution between heredity and environmental factors as determining longevity." It is better, he holds, to put more of the responsibility for health and long life on ourselves than on our chromosomes. Professor Drake writes that while there is "some scientific evidence that longevity runs in families," medical opinion also holds "that those who live long 'take care of themselves'" (*op. cit.*, p. 284). Dr. Stieglitz makes the important point that what seems to be hereditary influence may rather be "*familial influences*, including both the factors of genetic heredity and the habits formed by early childhood environment" (*op. cit.*, p. 44). He writes that obesity, for example, instead of being biologically inherited, may come from habits of heavy eating in the family.

This point, it seems to me, needs far more attention. It were well for those who come from relatively short-lived families to check their habits and customs against those of long-lived families. They should discuss their familial habits with their doctor. How we eat, drink, sleep, dress, work, and worry tends to affect our life span for good or bad. Though these factors are not inherited, they reflect familial influence and have effects which give the appearance of being inherited.

An Englishman, Sir James Crighton-Brown, who lived to be 97, is quoted as saying, "There is no short cut to longevity. To achieve it is the work of a lifetime" (*Time*, Oct. 20, 1958). Certainly, inheritance or no, longevity thrives on moderation and temperance in everything. If one said facetiously that the surest way to live long is to develop a stomach ailment early, one could make a case for it. At the 50th annual meeting of the American Public Health Association, a near-centenarian, Dr. Stephen Smith, clear-voiced at 98, said, "You all want to know the secret of my longevity. It is very simple. Do as I did a half century ago. Get yourself a heart impairment — not too serious — and take care of it!"[1]

The key to long life, if there is any at all, is taking care of oneself. This means taking care of one's body as the temple of one's soul by observing the spirit of the Ten Commandments. This spirit is moderation. A person driven by an uncongenial stomach or a spasmodic heart into moderation will usually out-live one with the constitution of the proverbial ox. Of Carlyle, who lived to be 86, we read that even before twenty-five he suffered "agonies from a gastric complaint which continued to torment him all his life." Of Fielding, on the other hand, we read that he was "Tall, strong, handsome," but that he "had led a wild youth, and he paid for it — he was an old man when he died at forty-seven." In about 1876 a girl in Detroit was certified as dead of typhoid fever. When her coffin was momentarily reopened, her eyelid was seen to move. She got well, and five years later became a Little Sister of the Poor. After a life of service, Sister Delphine de St. Paul Keuch died at 99! (Brooklyn *Tablet*, Dec. 27, 1958). After Cardinal Roncalli at 76 became Pope John XXIII, displaying a vigor and enthusiasm young men might envy, his sister, Assunta, coming to Rome for the corona-tion, brought some homemade sausages along for his Holiness. She explained, "His stomach has always been delicate and God knows what kind of food they give him here" (Philadelphia *Inquirer*, Nov. 6, 1959)!

For Americans, living in the land of bulging food surpluses, perhaps the most practical caution is not to eat too much. Pro-fessor Drake writes, "First, there is good reason to believe that a proper diet throughout infancy, childhood, and youth, and on

---

[1] Quoted from Julietta K. Arthur's *How to Help Older People* (Phila-delphia: J. B. Lippincott Co., 1954), p. 84.

into adulthood slows down the aging process" (*op. cit.*, p. 285). Proper diet, meaning first of all moderate, as well as regular and balanced, is the nearest thing to an elixir of youth we have. Dr. Shock writes, "Shortening of the life span by overfeeding has been demonstrated in silkworms and in a number of small aquatic animals. In rats and mice, restriction of caloric intake, beginning early in life, retards the growth rate, but extends the life span significantly" (*Trends In Research*, p. 126). As a matter of fact, rats restricted to about half their customary caloric intake, while "stunted in growth, lived much longer than their well-fed brothers and sisters." Mrs. Helen Doneger of the New York Institute of Dietetics says,

> Middle-aged Americans generally eat too much of the wrong kinds of food. They eat too much food of high caloric content — fried foods, rich gravies and sauces, rich desserts. They don't eat enough of the foods richest in protein, vitamins, and minerals — milk, fish, organ meats such as liver, green vegetables.[2]

Fewer calories and more proteins and vitamins are the prescription everywhere pressed upon us. Despite this, most men from forty to sixty still eat probably twice as much as they should, and many women, if they do not eat too much, eat fitfully and unevenly. For the longest life, one's weight should not be appreciably higher at fifty than it was at twenty-five. Experts call it unwise to grow in the middle after one has stopped growing at the top! They are also dogmatic in holding that fat people rarely have to worry about old age! Dr. Stieglitz writes, "Of 10 fat men at 30, 6 will survive to 60, 3 to 70, and perhaps 1 to 80; of 10 lean men, 2 will reach 60, 5 reach 70, and 3 will live out their second forty years" (*op. cit.*, p. 178).

He gives tables (pp. 175–176) showing the right weight range for men and women of every height and body frame. At twenty-five and all subsequent ages, the right weights for a few types are as follows:

---

[2] Quoted from Max Gunther's "A Vitality Diet for a Young Middle Age," *Coronet*, Dec., 1958.

height 5′ 2″ — frame, small   — weight range, 116–125 pounds
    frame, medium — weight range, 124–133 pounds
    frame, large   — weight range, 131–142 pounds
height 5′ 9″ — frame, small   — weight range, 140–151 pounds
    frame, medium — weight range, 149–160 pounds
    frame, large   — weight range, 157–170 pounds
height 6′ 3″ — frame, small   — weight range, 168–180 pounds
    frame, medium — weight range, 176–189 pounds
    frame, large   — weight range, 184–202 pounds

Correspondingly the right weights for several types of women are:

height 4′ 11″ — frame, small   — weight range, 104–111 pounds
    frame, medium — weight range, 110–118 pounds
    frame, large   — weight range, 117–127 pounds
height 5′ 6″ — frame, small   — weight range, 123–132 pounds
    frame, medium — weight range, 130–140 pounds
    frame, large   — weight range, 138–150 pounds
height 5′ 11″ — frame, small   — weight range, 139–150 pounds
    frame, medium — weight range, 148–158 pounds
    frame, large   — weight range, 155–169 pounds

For some of us these ideal weight ranges may look like Procrustean beds into which we will never fit — or only as shriveled heaps of skin and bones! But perhaps we can at least approximate them. Certainly all of us should try.

Doctors and gerontologists are not yet positive about the optimum weights or their importance. But they are firm in their contention that the only satisfactory way for all but the fewest abnormal cases to keep the weight right is to eat right. That means for most people eating less — habitually. It is harder work to walk off a pound than to fast it off. Dr. Peter J. Steincrohn, who writes that "You can't be fat and fit," declares, "If you want to reduce, the surest way to do it is by dieting. . . . As for exercise, you would have to walk about 36 miles to dissolve one pound of body fat" (*Live Longer and Enjoy It*, Prentice Hall, 1956, pp. 201–211). Fasting off weight gradually is far more reliable than starving it off and vastly safer than "fadding" it off. Reducing should be a gradual process, founded on sensible habits of eating less. Dramatic weight reductions — by means of starving, or fad diets, or reducing pills — are seldom lasting. Dr. Donald

Petit, nutrition authority, holds that "95% of all obese people" who diet or starve away pounds will in ten years be as fat as ever, while in the same time one third of all patients treated for cancer "remain free of new malignancies" (*Newsweek*, Sept. 1, 1958). Eating meals of normal variety but of smaller portions of everything is the sensible way of insuring weight reduction without the loss of important food ingredients and vitamins.

Anyone undertaking an unaccustomed program of weight-reduction should naturally do so under the guidance of a reputable physician. As somewhat of a guide for the proper daily calorie intake for proper nourishment at given ages and weights, the following list may be helpful.[3] Accordingly, for a "vitality" diet:

a girl,   15, weighing 108 pounds, needs 2600 calories a day
a boy,   15, weighing 108 pounds, needs 3100 calories a day
a woman, 25, weighing 128 pounds, needs 2300 calories a day
a man,   25, weighing 154 pounds, needs 3200 calories a day
a woman, 65, weighing 128 pounds, needs 1800 calories a day
a man,   65, weighing 154 pounds, needs 2552 calories a day

A boy needs the highest caloric intake of his life from 16 to 19, when one weighing 139 pounds should have 3600 calories a day. At 65, both men and women need fewer calories than at 25.

While the need for calories decreases after 25, the protein and vitamin needs remain about the same into the later years. In 1956 the U. S. Department of Agriculture published four groups of daily *must* foods for older people. They are: two cups of milk or some cheese or ice cream; two servings of meat, fish, poultry, or eggs; four or more servings of whole-grain, enriched or restored cereals or bread; and four or more servings of vegetables and fruits. The latter group should include: one serving of deep-green or deep-yellow vegetables every other day; one serving of citrus fruit or other fruit or vegetable containing Vitamin C (citrus, tomatoes, sweet peppers, cantaloupes, broccoli, strawberries, and many of the dark-green leafy vegetables); servings of other fruits and vegetables including potatoes. To these four

---

[3] This data is taken from Max Gunther's article, "A Vitality Diet for a Young Middle Age," *Coronet*, Dec., 1958, where the figures for more of the age groups are given than we have space for.

basic groups may be added, as taste and circumstances require, butter, margarine, other fats, oils, sugar, syrup and enriched cereal products.[4]

While most people certainly in the middle years and some also in the later must be cautioned not to eat too much, gerontologists do find that some older people, especially those living alone, eat too little and too monotonously. In the later years, what with a weakened sense of taste, lack of exercise and of table companions, people sometimes have an irregular appetite. If furthermore they are on a restricted budget, they may slump into a "bread and potato" diet. They skip some meals entirely, and at others eat only starch and virtually no proteins or vitamin-containing foods. In this matter of eating, as in most other necessities of life, we should acquire right and regular habits as early as possible and stick to them. Unless markedly unwell, when it is time to eat we should make an effort to eat what common sense or the doctor tells us to eat. If we must save, we should do it elsewhere, not on proper nutrition.

Older people also need to be cautioned against faddist tendencies. When age weakens one, it is only natural to be tempted by the promises of quacks and food faddists. The best of us have a lingering trust in these. But reputable dietitians and doctors universally discourage, and often flatly condemn them. Dr. Frederick J. Stare, chairman of the Department of Nutrition, Harvard University School of Public Health, said, "It is surprising and pathetic to witness how eagerly concoctions hinting at the elixir of youth are sought by the older generation."

Some ten million Americans spend annually about $500,000,000 on "'wonder foods,' vitamins, and minerals" (*Newsweek*, Sept. 15, 1959). Some of these people are called food faddists who to

---

[4] *Health Guide* for Institutions Serving Older People (Division of Aging, Health and Welfare Council, Philadelphia, 1958) gives some explanation of this food plan and also lists "Special Diets," to be given only under doctor's orders: diebetic, low-sodium, low-fat, and soft diet (pp. 20–24).

The manual, *Standards of Care for Older People in Institutions* (The National Committee of the Aging, 345 E. 46th St., New York 17, 1953, 112 pp.) in Chapter III, "Food and Food Service" gives helpful hints on the nutritional needs of older people.

create attention want to eat peculiar things. But also many are older people who can least afford it, who are taken in by quack promises of rejuvenating vigor. In most of these foods, according to *Newsweek*, "the carefully labeled ingredients in the nostrums are, in themselves, harmless. Supplementary vitamins, dehydrated potatoes and cucumbers and onions and 'natural foods' raised by organic farming can neither help nor harm the average well nourished American." When Dr. Shock was asked, "What about the fad diets — blackstrap molasses and yogurt, things of that sort?" he replied "that in general the limitation of diet to single items or groups in the long run is bad. The yogurt story really has never been adequately explored." This leaves a straw of hope for the yogurt enthusiasts! As regards vitamins, admittedly important, he said, ". . . the best source of vitamins is the grocery store, not the drug store" (*U.S. News*, Oct. 23, 1953). As for vegetarianism, I do not find it especially condemned anywhere, but certainly not commended either. Since, however, virtually all the prescribed diets include meat or fish, it would seem to be disapproved by implication. But because Bernard Shaw was not only a vegetarian but one of the greatest playwrights of our time, I content myself with saying that if vegetarianism has no special virtues, it has the general one of keeping its devotees from over-eating!

Fads and nostrums, according to the doctors, most often do their harm indirectly in causing people to neglect proper medical treatment, especially if they have diseases of the nerves, blood, liver, kidneys, heart, or digestive tracts. The best general advice to people is that they should eat the customary foods in varied but modest proportions. Other than that, except for perhaps annual medical examinations, they should not be preoccupied with their stomach. Constant worry about food, stomach, and about bowel movements is one mark of senility! As Hamlet said to the players, "Pray you, avoid it!" Let the Lord and the doctor do the worrying.

Happily the doctors are not as unanimous against any and all alcohol as they seem to be against food fads. Regular alcoholics, of course have little cause to be concerned about old age. They tend to be spared that stage of life, though it is not certain whether their being spared is due to the embalming properties of alcohol or to the deficiency of proteins and vitamins drinking tends to cause.[5] As for moderate drinking, doctors and geriatricians seem rather to approve than condemn it. They condone, almost commend a social cocktail or two or a highball, a glass or two of wine or beer before, during, or after meals. It is as if the experts were heeding Ecclesiasticus, who, while condemning wine drunken to excess as raising "quarrels, and wrath, and many ruins," affirmed that "Wine was created from the beginning to make men joyful, and not to make them drunk. . . . Sober drinking is health to soul and body" (35–38).

In the forties, Dr. Clendening, referred to above (in Chapter III), shocked Kansas by declaring that "what the country needed was a good 5¢ shot of whiskey" (*Time*, Feb. 12, 1945). Recent investigators discovered that "The alcohol in a cocktail or two doesn't put as much of a load on the heart as the adrenalin produced under conditions of stress" (*U. S. News*, Sept. 5, 1958). In fact these and other health specialists tend to confirm, at least for people over forty, the latter half of St. Paul's prescription to Timothy: "Do not still drink water, but use a little wine for thy stomach's sake" (Timothy 3:8). One rejoices that this biblical high water mark of concession to human nature has so far found favor with the geriatricians. Dr. Shock said, ". . . many physicians find that a little bit of alcohol is a very useful tonic for older people." He thought a couple of ounces of whisky before dinner, that sort of thing, "would be O.K." He quoted Dr. William Stroud's making the headlines some years ago "when he stated that before the age of forty alcohol was poison and after

---

[5] In an article entitled, "How Long Will You Live" (*Catholic Digest*, Jan., 1953), Paul Green writes, "Heavy drinkers (who consume a pint a day on the average and are drunk once a week or so) are likely to suffer from diabetes, high blood pressure, cirrhosis of the liver, neuritis, gout and Bright's disease, all of which shorten life. Confirmed alcoholics (drunk almost daily and regularly almost insensibly drunk) invite early death because of malnutrition, which makes them susceptible to disease, particularly pneumonia."

40 it was a necessity." He concluded, "I think it is useful for older people in small amounts" (*U.S. News*, Oct. 23, 1953).

The researchers who evaluated the strain of a cocktail on the heart, quoted above, also found that "By dilating peripheral arteries, alcohol may help the heart pump more efficiently," but quickly add that "it cannot be said that liquor will greatly improve the lot of the heart"! Dr. Stieglitz said that of ninety nonagenarians interviewed, "Some are teetotalers and others go to the other extreme and feel they never would have survived without their daily toddies." He concluded, "Using alcohol does not seem to affect the life span — if we really mean use, not abuse" (*U.S. News*, Feb. 14, 1958). While I subconsciously suspect that the experts are overgenerous toward alcohol, I never protest when either the theologians or the physicians give human nature a break! Except to warn that alcohol can in the best of us most insidiously lead to abuse, and is furthermore unhappily expensive, we are glad of its qualified approval.

Smoking comes off much worse at the hands of the health experts. Also, we note, it does not get support from the Bible! The last years have seen somewhat of a pitched battle between cigarette interests and lung and cancer specialists. So far nobody has tried to argue that smoking, if we except the sheer pleasure of it, does anybody any good, and many have argued that it does considerable harm, especially in the form of cigarettes. But the harm has not yet been conclusively established in kind and degree. Dr. Shock said that as regards lung cancer, he will stick to a pipe and take his chances, "But certainly individuals with circulation diseases in the extremities — and they can be identified — have got to quit smoking" (*U.S. News*, Oct. 23, 1953). Dr. Stieglitz said, "Data indicates that there exists some relationship between cancer of the lungs and smoking." Also, smokers more than nonsmokers develop high blood pressure. He summarized the matter as follows:

> There are great individual variations. We hear of men who have smoked 20 'stogies' a day for 50 years and we can't find evidence that it does them any damage (*U. S. News*, Feb. 14, 1958).

He said he himself started smoking cigarettes in 1913, and stopping now would be too late to undo what damage if any was done. Economically speaking, smoking is an expensive vice which biologically does no good and often does at least some harm. There is no valid reason for not giving it up — except the nature of human nature! As Mark Twain so graphically put it: "Habit is habit, and not to be flung out of the window by any man, but coaxed downstairs a step at a time." The longer we have had the habit of smoking the harder it is to give up. It cannot be justified biologically or economically, yet in moderation it may for many have a valid psychical, emotional justification. For them, as Ecclesiasticus justifyingly said of wine, it "is joy to the soul and the heart." As to moderation, Dr. Boas writes that people suffering from narrowed arteries of the legs, chronic bronchitis, asthma, chronic sinus infection, and those who develop dizziness should stop smoking. But most others, he writes, "can smoke with impunity." But he hastily urges moderation even for them: "Of course, it is best to keep the consumption down to ten or fifteen cigarettes, or two or three cigars, or a half-dozen pipefuls a day" (*op. cit.*, p. 36).

After proper eating and avoidance of vices, the most important factor for long life is adequate sleep. Because it comes so naturally, possibly not enough attention has been given to it. Many a constitution is probably undermined in the twenties by long hours of night life and short hours of slumber. An infant sleeps twenty hours, a child ten, a young person should sleep eight. Middle-agers need only six or seven hours, but those in the later years should in addition to the six or seven take one or two short naps during the day. A twenty-minute nap after meals is worth an hour or more at night. Sleep, including such naps, is the miracle "drug" of most great men. The round numbers here recommended of course admit of individual variations.

In the later years of reduced exercise, the need for sleep often seems less. It therefore becomes all the more urgent to heed any signals of fatigue and get some rest. Possibly because of inadequate exercise, oldsters often are troubled by insomnia. Just when they finally have enough time to sleep, they seem unable to. While with a doctor's approval sleeping pills may be taken, they should not be either the first or the habitual recourse. It is better to try a change of habits and circumstances. Perhaps retiring later, elimination of disturbances and a change in food or drink may prove helpful. Some people, for example, find a warm glass of milk sweetened with honey before retiring an aid to sleep. It is well to find the best time for our rest and then as much as possible to make that habitual. We should by all means push unpleasant thoughts into the background and think of pleasant, wholesome things as we retire. For many of us, a bit of light but elevating reading proves fine, like a chapter of the familiar Bible stories. For some a prolonging of their night prayers works magic. I myself find saying the rosary (not on my knees but in bed) the best preparation for sleep. What I myself find hard is not to fret when on occasion I do not fall asleep or if I wake up after a couple of hours. Such fretting is poison. Just resting resignedly, when nature or God denies us sleep on occasion, can be quite refreshing of itself. Those lazy moments should be used for pleasant planning, pious meditation, or some extra decades of the rosary.

Fundamentally, the best way to better sleep is enough exercise. Dr. Boas writes, "Every man and woman, even in the seventh and eighth decade, if physically sound, should take some form of regular exercise daily" (*op. cit.*, p. 20). He names walking, golf, swimming, dancing, setting-up exercises, light gardening, and woodcutting. Someone pointed out that after their exile, Napoleon lived only six years, Louis Philippe only two, Napoleon III only three, but Kaiser Wilhelm II, who after his exile from Germany to Holland, became known as "The Woodchopper of Doorn," lived on for 23 years, one fourth of his life. In our time Chancellor Konrad Adenauer of West Germany, 83 on January 5, 1959, who for ten years has been leading his nation from chaos to prosperity, takes a daily walk. In rain, shine, or snow, accompanied by State Secretary Hans Globke, himself 60, he takes a two-mile stroll, a *Spaziergang*, every afternoon, to the slopes of the Rhine.

Of all forms of exercise the German *Spaziergang* is the one most deserving of wider cultivation in America. It could help us not only get older more healthfully but to enjoy our later years more. Among sports, the more competitive ones, such as tennis and handball, are less desirable than golf, archery, and bowling. Activities involving sudden explosions of energy like heavy lifting, running for a train, pushing a wheelbarrow up a hill, should be avoided. But restrained activity, whether for sport or for getting things done around the house or elsewhere, is necessary for healthful living. For any form of work or sport, Dr. Stieglitz writes, it is not so much "what is done as how it is carried out. Even the patient with a severe heart disease can climb stairs — if he does it slowly" (*op. cit.,* p. 267).

If work and exercise are needed to keep us fit in the later years, personal hygiene and good grooming are needed to make our staying alive worthwhile for ourselves and our neighbors. In our day and age it is assumed that people in the later years will wash and bathe and keep their clothes clean. But they should also keep their clothes in fashion, up-to-date. Women should continue any sensible "beauty" treatments. Men should not only keep their hair cut and combed, but if they shaved daily before retirement they should continue to do so. A morning shave acts like a tonic.

Keeping fit requires character and will power. At seventy one does not stand straight or walk firmly unless one is determined to do so. In "Don't Let Age Creep Up on You," Columnist Josephine Lowman, trying to analyze what it really was that made a mother look older than the daughter, found it to be more than wrinkles; it was posture: "The mother slumped some, her head protruded a little, and her abdomen was thickened." In walking, "The mother's movements were stiff," and lacked elasticity and grace (Philadelphia *Bulletin*, July 1, 1958).

One must not only *will* to live long, one must work at it. Dr. C. Ward Crampton, in "Live Long and Like It" (Public Affairs

Pamphlet No. 139, 1948) urges those who want to live long and like it, among other things, to hold their head high and back straight, to stand tall, and to keep their abdomen flat.

Eventually in the course of nature the best of us may sag and shuffle. But unless as a matter of will and character we cultivate the habit of standing tall and walking straight we will slump into a heap of decrepitude sooner than God and nature intended. Ever so often, as a matter of principle, we should get our old body into our Sunday shirt, suit, and shoes, and walk forth into the open sky, thanking God we are still alive. The Catholic commandment to attend Mass every Sunday, properly attired, is a splendid thing, not only for eventually getting to heaven, but also in at least some part for achieving the maximum life expectancy.

CHAPTER VI

Meeting the Ills of the Body

HOWEVER luckily we may reach or surpass the life expectancy destined for us, we can hardly hope to do so without a goodly share of aches and pains. When the Psalmist moaned that what is more than fourscore years is "labor and sorrow," he merely recognized that the longer we live the more is likely to be our share of accidents, viruses, and chronic impairments. The gerontologists rightly have it as their ideal to make the later years reasonably healthy rather than ailingly longer. Once again one can only reflect that at best the later years with their thinning hair, their loss of teeth, their diminishing vision, their impaired hearing, their wrinkles and rheumatisms can only be properly justified and appreciated as a gradual transition from the natural man to the spiritual one. In this light we should regard what infirmities may be visited on us in the later years. We should accept them bravely if we must, yet also avail ourselves of the best that care and medicine can do to prevent, or postpone, or moderate them.

When science provides ameliorations of the impairments of age, we should use them. When the eyes weaken, we should get them fitted with proper glasses — and wear them. When hearing fails, we should, if possible, get a hearing aid. We owe it not only to ourselves but to our relatives and neighbors to keep our hearing as efficient as possible. Faulty hearing makes for misunderstandings and aggravates a certain suspiciousness to which oldsters unhappily are prone. Perhaps even more important, for our appearance and our nutrition, are our teeth. No stomach is strong enough for a jaw that doesn't chew. If a tooth falls out, we should get it replaced. If all decay, we should have a denture made and keep using it with a will — until we feel and look natural with it.

We must guard our limbs. Partly because of various impairments of the senses, partly because of general stiffness and brittleness, we are especially prone to accidents in the later years. They become frequent after 45, multiple at 65. Bernard Shaw, the hardy vegetarian whom illness could not lay low, succumbed to accidents. In 1946, falling from a chair, he said,

> When one is very old, as I am, one of the unpleasant things seems to be that your legs give in before your head does, and secondly, you are always stumbling about. I tumble down about three times a week quite regularly.

In 1950, at 94, while cutting the limb off a tree in his garden, he fell again and fractured his left thighbone. This required an operation, which he did not long outlive. In the later years, just when failing eyes and faltering legs endanger our steps, our bones, too, and tissues heal much more slowly, so that full recovery may become problematic. Therefore, surely, a moment of care can prevent a month of cure. When we get older, we simply must think before we act, look before we step, grab a railing before we go up or down. If there is anything best delegated to juniors, it is standing on ladders and washing windows!

In addition to the accident hazards and the degenerative factors which predispose to them, older people are subject to most of the infections and viruses which trouble everybody. Furthermore they are inclined to several categories of chronic ailments peculiar to age or aggravated by it. In fact, writing this during an acute attack of gout, I am inclined to reflect that the Lord allows the later years so that the sundry plagues ordained for mankind after Adam's Fall can be visited in full on a maximum of individuals in person! Statistically, the later years figure ominously healthwise.

According to two health surveys between 1935 and 1943, "persons aged 65 or over had almost twice as many disabling illnesses lasting a week, or longer, as persons aged 15–64 . . . the average disabling illness of the aged lasted twice as long as that of the younger group" (see Corson and McConnell, *op. cit.*, p. 21). For what consolation it may be, "Informed opinion holds that brief illnesses — incapacitating the individual for less than a week — are less prevalent among the aged than among the young groups." But this consolation is at once dimmed by another informed opinion. Corson and McConnell continue:

> Among persons over 64, it is estimated, from one tenth to one third are chronically ill. About one half of all chronically ill persons are over age 45, and most persons over 60 have some more or less permanent disability or disease (*op. cit.*, p. 21).

Fortunately these figures have been attacked as exaggerated, but it is considered "clear that at any one time a substantial proportion of the aged are chronically ill." The New Jersey Old Age Study Commission, explaining "that the number one economic burden of old age — to society and to many individuals — is ill health," states, "Almost one-half of all persons over 65 in the United States has a chronic disease or impairment" (*A Positive Policy Toward Aging*, Feb., 1957).

Professor Drake gives Public Health Service figures to the effect that in 1950 two million of the twelve million people 65 and over had a long-term disability, defined as one lasting for three months or more. That is 17 per cent. Of the 5,289,060 persons in the country who had such a long-term disability, "Those over 65 and over constituted nearly 40 per cent of all those classified" (*op. cit.*, p. 293). A survey in Hagerstown, Maryland, by the U. S. Health Service probably conveys the fairest picture:

> At 25 about 35 of every 1,000 persons have some chronic illness (heart disease, ulcers, diabetes, cancer) or some major physical disability, chiefly accidents. At 45, the rate gradually rises to about 100 chronic cases in 1,000 men and women. After that, there is a much steeper climb, with nearly 250 out of 1,000 chronically ill at 60. At 80, more than half the group needed regular medical care, and at 90, the rate is more than 900 per 1000.

Those figures, while indicating a lot of personal suffering and a terrific economic strain, do not fortunately consign the majority of us to invalidism. As Dr. Shock points out, "we can say with assurance . . . that there are a large number of individuals beyond the age 65 who remain relatively healthy and who are still able to perform effectively in daily living" (*Trends in Gerontology*, p. 49). A distinction should be made between *impairment*, some of which almost everybody suffers, and *disability*. According to one national health survey, although between 65 and 75 half were impaired, only 5 per cent were disabled; between 75 and 84, 60 per cent were impaired, but only 10 per cent were disabled (see *Trends*, p. 47).

While therefore chronic total invalidism is a frightening calamity, it strikes a small enough percentage to justify the hope in each of us of being mercifully spared this cross. If there is one plea we should include in our prayers for ourselves and for our loved ones, it is that God may see fit to spare us and them of total chronic invalidism. Or if we are not to be spared, that He may mercifully soon call us home to Him. Yet in this too His will be done. A grandfather of mine (whom I did not personally know) became, following an accident, a bedridden invalid for seven years before he died at seventy. Surely his invalidism was not only hard on him, but for seven years held the whole family in the anguish that comes from seeing someone in pain. Yet when my mother and uncles and aunts describe the period of their father's taxing illness, one cannot help getting the impression that it was for all of them a valuable spiritual experience. For grandfather himself, the suffering which he endured bravely and resignedly no doubt earned for him rich spiritual bonuses and eased his passage through purgatory into heaven. Surely, if one is man enough for it, it is better and more meritorious to do one's suffering here on earth for the sins even the best of us commits than in purgatory, where there are no loved ones to tend us or doctors to alleviate the pain. Happily, modern medicine can spare us the sort of prolonged excruciating pain that in former ages could drive sufferers to blaspheming, and often literally drove them mad. For that means of relief which Christian culture produced as a by-product of its general beneficence we can be everlastingly grateful.

When in any family, someone becomes a chronic invalid, his care becomes a major project for the family or the community. The details of such care cannot be blueprinted here in general terms. With the help of the family doctor, the pastor, the local health services, the best methods for handling and financing the case must be worked out.

In the meantime, all of us who reach the later years, even though spared the worst, must be prepared for a goodly share of aches and pains. We will continue to be subject to most of the infections and viruses of our younger days and become predisposed to a grim assortment of possible chronic degenerative plagues. As for the infectious diseases, modern medicine has reduced their danger considerably. Pneumonia, once a scourge for the elderly, has been restrained by antibiotic drugs. The common cold however still flourishes in undiminished vigor, which aspirins and antihistamines can somewhat relieve as to symptoms and severity but not as to duration. Dr. Boas writes that old people can expect several colds a year, just as when younger, but they do not shake them off as readily. The head cold, whose virus is still immune to known drugs, invites secondary infection — sinusitis, bronchitis, and bronchopneumonia. To prevent these, "it is well for older persons to receive penicillin or other antibiotics as soon as they develop a cold" (*op. cit.*, p. 188).

The various infectious diseases such as diphtheria, typhoid, chicken pox, syphilis, tuberculosis are always due to some kind of bacteria. Their onset, except in tuberculosis, is usually violent, their diagnosis certain, and their course either fatal or their cure complete. Most of the illnesses of youth are of that kind. They come from without, and can be controlled by quarantines.

But the disorders of senescence are not infective, they arise from within the body, and have complex causes. Even when they are diagnosed for what they are, the far more important and difficult matter is to discover why they came about. Furthermore, they develop insidiously, silently, and may have sabotaged our system for years before they produce pains that lead to their discovery.

As regards health, people seem to fall into several categories. Some are overanxious. They go around most of their lives moaning about their poor health. They display a "morbid anxiety about health, with no physical signs of disease." They are especially inclined to fancy pains in the chest. They are described in the article, "Hypochondriacs at Large" (*Catholic Digest*, May, 1959). These psychosomatic unfortunates recall a Harvard dean's answer to a student who had justified his missing assignment with the excuse, "I wasn't feeling very well, sir." The late Dean Briggs said,

> Mr. Smith, I think that in time you may perhaps find that most of the work of the world was done by people who aren't feeling very well.

Frederick Lewis Allen's comment on this is:

> The Dean knew that there is such a thing as a sensibly prudent attitude toward one's health. But he also knew that the symptoms of fatigue and of laziness are practically identical; that it is hard to tell the difference between not feeling well and not feeling like doing a hard job (quoted in *Reader's Digest*, Mar., 1953).

Far more conducive to long life and high enterprise is the attitude implied in the answer George Bernard Shaw gave when, in his eighties, he was asked how he felt: "At my age, you either feel all right or you are dead."

Those of the second category are the bumptiously healthy. They tend to thump their chest and say, "I don't feel a day older than twenty." They cry, "You're as old as you feel, and I feel as fit as forty." In this bravado there is an unconvincing ring. It symptomizes an ostrich-like refusal to accept old age and may harm in two ways. It often tempts people into over-exertion and unwise competitive activities; and it makes them allergic to medical examinations and blind to telltale symptoms.

Often when those who were long bumptious about their health do succumb to a chronic illness which has sneaked up on them, they lapse into a third category: those who capitalize on their ailment. Dr. Boas speaks of some who "become very skillful in using their disabilities to maintain domination over their children" (*op. cit.*, p. 242). They tend to fall into one of the most obnoxious pitfalls of old age: that of talking about their ailment in and out of season. To get the sympathy they crave, they encourage being waited on, rather than doing for themselves everything which their doctor thinks they can do. This hurts their well-being even more than it strains their relatives. The patient, for example, who services his colostomy himself will be much the better for it than depending on others.

The sensibly prudent attitude toward our health is not to be on the prowl for chronic ailments but to realize that we may have them before we feel them. Hypertension, gout, arteriosclerosis, and chronic joint disorders have their most frequent beginnings between forty and sixty. The most common onset of diabetes is in the sixth decade, nearly five per cent of those over forty-five have it. Especially in older persons, it develops so insidiously that it is often not discovered until a routine examination for some other disturbance uncovers it.

A sensibly prudent attitude toward our health in the later years would therefore include a professional friendly relationship with a good doctor, who knows our own and our family's background, with whom we are relaxed, and whose routine checking and testing is supplemented by his friendly intuition. Most health authorities strongly urge at least one routine checkup a year. While one cannot absolutely rely on such routine checkups, still they are likely to uncover the worst danger signals and show the urgency of a thorough examination in a hospital or health clinic. Happily every year, in fact every month, the diagnostic devices for detecting chronic illness are improving, along with their cure or easement.[1]

---

[1] A lay person can himself procure any of several health inventories, with the aid of which if properly filled out any doctor or hospital can more quickly and accurately make diagnosis. One such is "Columbia Adult Health Inventory," by Irving Lorge, Jacob Tuckerman, and Frederick D. Zeman, 1953, Institute of Psychological Research, Columbia University, New York City (5 cents a copy). Its 180 questions take about 25 minutes to answer.

Fortunately too we become somewhat less susceptible to pain as we grow older. Perhaps it is Nature's gesture of compensation for the multitudinous chronic ills encompassing the later years. It is as if we slowly got used to aches and discomforts. Dr. Stieglitz writes, "The sense of pain is dulled in the aging and especially in the aged" (*op. cit.,* p. 82). Surely to be assured that our terminal sickness will hurt less at eighty than had we died at forty is a modest comfort! Yet, as Dr. Stieglitz and others point out, it is a mixed blessing. A youth with appendicitis will suffer enough to start an ambulance; but the aged think of it as a minor stomach upset until it is ruptured. All this means that while we should certainly on no account start spying on our organs for signs of distress, we should be alert to any new discomforts and let a doctor evaluate them. After that we should follow his instructions conscientiously, but let him do the worrying. Our worrying never helps. If perchance we insist on worrying about pains the doctor cannot locate or dismisses as not dangerous, we become candidates for senility.

The chronic diseases of the later years, which may sabotage long before they hurt, are silent in their approach, and complex in their causes. We must therefore avail ourselves of the best diagnostic devices of modern medicine to spot them as early as possible. Most of them if spotted early can be reduced in intensity and rapidity of development, but many of them also can be checked. Many a small growth can be excised before it has become a tumor!

Next to their silent development and complex causes the chronic ailments are progressive. They do not just come and go. They come and get worse — unless something from outside the body, surgery or antibiotics or serums — is effectively rushed against them. We may positively not assume in the later years that a persistent pain in the joints will politely disappear without medication, or that blood in the stool is just a passing fancy of nature. We must have the phenomenon properly diagnosed. We

---

Another is "The Cornell Medical Index," Cornell University Medical College, 1300 York Ave., New York 31 (10 cents a copy).

should have a physician who is as perspicacious and wise as he is skillful. However, it may ease our minds to reflect that while a doctor's false diagnosis in the young may easily be fatal, in the elder, excepting heart trouble, it is seldom fatal, only exasperating and painful! In Nature's curious method of compensation, the chronic ailments of the later years do not gallup, they creep: they give us plenty time to come to know them familiarly!

These chronic ailments which like termites threaten wrinkled bodies fall into three classes. Dr. Morris Fishbein in "Health in the Later Years" summarizes them as follows:

> the fatalities arise from heart disease, kidney disease, hardening of the arteries, and cancer. The disabilities are associated with such conditions as diabetes and the greatest of all causes of disability, arthritis and rheumatism.[2]

He alludes to some of the intensive research that is being done, specifically on the hardening of the arteries causing parkinsonism or the shaking palsy, on the functioning and possible deficiencies of such glands as the sex, adrenal, thyroid, and pituitary, and on the dryness or pigmentation of the skin which causes itching. He states that at present the leading cause of death is heart disease, including coronary thrombosis, the second is hyptertension or high blood pressure, and the third is cancer. He throws out this hope:

> Now all of these conditions are under investigation and those who are experts in the field and associated with leading institutions of research. . . . American Heart Association, American Association of High Blood Pressure, American Cancer Society, and similar groups — all look forward to the conquering of these conditions in the not too distant future . . . (*op. cit.*, p. 80).

Dr. Stieglitz in an interview (*U. S. News*, Feb. 14, 1958) called the "chronic progressive disorders which beset our aging" the major health problem. Of three general types, he lists "the cardiovascular disorders, high blood pressure and arteriosclerosis" as the worst, accounting for half "of all deaths in the United

---

[2] In *Good News for Later Life*, New York State Joint Legislative Committee on Problems of the Aging, 1958, p. 79.

States today. Arteriosclerosis furthermore is the cause of confused dementia." As the second group he lists "metabolic disorders — diabetes, pernicious anemia, thyroid deficiencies, sex-gland deficiences, gout, and forms of arthritis." The third one is cancer, preferably written "cancers."

Whereas the infectious diseases can be traced to a specific bacillus or a germ, these three types of disorders usually are "due to an accumulation of many factors which may vary in different individuals." Anyone looking for *the cause* of high blood pressure or of cancer, as if it were only one, is doomed to failure.

Luckily, however, even now a great many of these chronic plagues can be controlled and made virtually painless. One need merely cite the easement that has occurred for diabetes sufferers. My own chronic trouble, gout, once the terror of the English squire, is now much tamed by colchicine, benemid, zoxazolamine, and sulfinpyrazone. Only this spring, a method for giving colchicine intravenously was developed. Tomorrow, arthritis and bursitis may similarly come under the control of effective drugs. Where hitherto only one in four cancer patients could be saved to survive five or more years, it is now three (*Time*, July 27, 1959). Newell Brown, Chairman, Federal Council on Aging, has with good reason said that "we have made more progress in medical science in the last 50 years than in the previous 5,000. These advances are coming at a constantly accelerating rate" (New York State Committee, *op. cit.*, p. 146).

There is certainly a tremendous acceleration in medical progress. Medical researchers and geriatricians in some ten different countries, experimenting in hospitals, universities, and government laboratories, seem to be advancing concertedly upon the chronic disorders of the later years. They display the same energy and more of the enthusiasm of the scientists who work on intercontinental and interplanetary bombs and missiles. One senses almost a fever of experiment and research. The excitement that the early explorers registered for new continents now can be sensed behind the scholarly reports of medical progress. The exuberant energy of the researchers appears from an item in U. S. *News* entitled, "Fight on Disease — Some New Advances" (May 4, 1959). It refers to a new enzyme for blood clots (Plasmin, JB 516), a new drug for arthritis (dexamethasone), and a new tranquilizer and antidepressive for mental illness. It continues:

> Cancer — Some 70 compounds, out of 40,000 screened yearly in a search for a chemical cure, look promising enough to be given clinical trials in human beings. Progress is being made towards a simple test to detect cancer in its earliest stage.

George B. Stone, manager of a division of the Chas. Pfizer and Company Pharmaceutical manufacturer, is cited as predicting a breakthrough against arthritis, a vaccine against the common cold, and an effective new drug for heart disease all by 1962; and by 1965 a new cancer therapy, which will spectacularly reduce the cancer death rate by 1975 (U. S. *News*, Feb. 17, 1959).

While these predictions may be overoptimistic, they are nevertheless encouraging. In the cure of chronic illnesses, where wishful thinking is especially vivid, there are bound to be many disappointments and false hopes for many of us before, if ever, we find relief. But we can almost predict with certainty that if we live long enough either a check or at least a control for our personal ailment, if we have or get one, will be discovered. In the meanwhile we can hope and pray that it will be in time to do us some good.

We should also in the meanwhile take proper precautions against falling victims to quacks. While hope springs eternal and most improbably, especially in pain, still it would seem obvious that if a cure or control of our personal disorder had been discovered anywhere by anyone whatsoever, the whole world would know of it as soon as we, and all the drugstores would sell it. In the later years our medical expenses are likely to be large enough not to have them multiplied by quacks or peddlers of patent medicines.

Nor should we feel that because we have a chronic illness life is unendurable. Even chronic disorders of the worst kind do not usually rage all the time. Many of them strike only once or twice a year. Furthermore, something in our nature plus medical means will very likely reduce any pain to a point where it will become more and more endurable. From a merely natural point of view the mere thought of chronic illness is unendurable. But from the spiritual one, once we fix our eyes on Christ the Crucified, and reflect on the real purpose of our life here below, any chronic illness with all its pains and trials can be offered up to God for the richest of rewards.

In that spirit the chronically ill can resignedly and heroically go on living as fully and usefully as possible. In 1957, Dr. C. M. Hincks, founder of the Canadian Mental Health Association, wrote:

> Good health, while it is desirable, need not necessarily in all cases be an essential for rich living between 65 and 90 years of age. I have friends who have a lot of things wrong with them but who are living very full lives after 65. One is our greatest Canadian orator, who has arthritis and diabetes. Another is one of the most beloved women in Toronto, who has been operated upon for double cataract, who has arthritis, and who recently published her fascinating autobiography (*Aging Is Everyone's Concern*, First Ontario Conference on Aging, p. 2).

A recent headline, "Arthritic Nun Wins Craft Exhibit" (Brooklyn *Tablet*, Sept. 12, 1959) graphically illustrates Dr. Hincks's point. Sister Vincent of Foligno, Sisters of Charity of Providence, Seattle, has suffered for ten years from rheumatoid arthritis. But lying on her back, she modeled a figurine of St. Francis surrounded by birds and small animals which in her sixty-fourth year won her a top award at a state-wide ceramic and hobby show.

All Americans who almost weekly see pictures of the Secretary of State, Christian S. Herter, going off to foreign capitals, carrying a brief case under one arm for his facts and a crutch under the other for his arthritis, have an edifying proof that life can be worthwhile, though chronically afflicted. Catholics who know how gratefully many saints suffered the pangs of their stigmata for years and years can at least vaguely realize that pain and suffering are something mysteriously a part of God's plan, something we must in any case bear and should do so prayerfully.

CHAPTER VII

Keeping the Mind Fit

FOR most thoughtful persons, the prospect of physical decline and illness in the later years is far less disturbing than that of mental deterioration and childishness. For me personally, and probably for many others, the chief terror of old age has been, first, the proverbially alleged fading of mental ability, and second, the possibility of senility. For me, the chief value of doing the so-called research for this book has happily been the assurance of science and medicine that learning power for most people is virtually as good at sixty as at twenty, and may still be excellent at eighty. Likewise, mental breakdown — senile psychosis and cerebral arteriosclerosis — strike only perhaps five in a hundred and could in some of those cases have been prevented with wise living and sensible precautions.

There are convincing proofs that for the majority of us, while our bodies tend to slow down, our minds, including our memories, retain an amazing efficiency for both old and new intellectual activities. In Chapter II some instances were given of big and little people who late in life had the capacity and the will to acquire a new skill, to learn a new trade, or to adopt a new vocation. These instances evidence the capacity in the later years to adapt ourselves to altered conditions and to new trades and vocations.

As for high degrees of excellence in performance in one's life-long vocation, history abounds in illustrious examples of great achievement in the later years. Cervantes wrote the second part of his Don Quixote at 68, Goethe the second part of Faust at 80, and Tolstoy finished his *Resurrection* at 72 and his *The Law of Love and the Law of Violence* at 80. Tintoretto at 74 painted the *Paradise*, a grand canvas 74 feet by 30; Michelangelo started his Rondanimi *Pietá* at 80 and worked on until his death at 89; and Titian painted the *Battle of Lepanto* at 98. Verdi at 75 composed his masterpiece *Othello*, at 80 his *Falstaff*, and at 85 his universally popular "Ave Maria," "Stabat Mater," and "Te Deum." Lamarck at 78 completed his greatest zoological work, *The Natural History of the Invertebrates*; Kant at 74 wrote his *Anthropology* and his *Metaphysics of Ethics*. Holmes at 79 wrote *Over the Teacups*, Tennyson at 83 his "Crossing the Bar," and Edmund Waller at 79 his *Divine Poems*. Voltaire attended the first performance of his *Irené* at 84; Bernard Shaw wrote his masterpiece, *Saint Joan*, at 67 and his last play, *Bouyant Bullions*, at 91. Stradivarius made violins until he was 93; Sibelius composed at 82. Clemenceau at almost 78 dominated the Versailles Peace Treaty. Von Moltke at 88 was still chief of staff of the Prussian army; von Hindenburg was retired at 64, recalled in 1914 at 67 to defeat the Russians at Tannenberg, at 78 was elected president of the Weimar Republic, and in 1932 at 85 defeated Hitler at the polls for a second term as president.

When Alaska was admitted into the Union in 1958, Robert Service, laureate of the Yukon, at 84 commemorated the event with a verse entitled "Sourdough Star." When the late Frank Lloyd Wright at 83 was asked which of his works he would select as his masterpiece, he replied, "My next one." In 1958, at 81, Mary Garden slipped into Paris, where she had begun her singing career 58 years ago, "signed contracts for a film and television series based on her life, and made arrangements for a personal-appearance tour in the U. S. next January" (*Newsweek*, Sept. 8, 1958).

From every walk of life one could list contemporary examples of people who are not only stretching the average life span but running circles around most youngsters in mental alertness and energy. Dr. Charles G. Abbott, astrophysicist, from 1922 to 1944 secretary of the Smithsonian Institution, published his autobiography at 86, and in 1958 still rose at 7 and began his weather computations right after breakfast. As his recipe for living he declared, "I use the tops of my bifocal lenses to see the girls in the church choir, and the bottoms to read" (*Newsweek*, Sept. 29, 1958). Former President Herbert Hoover, who on his 84th birthday recommended fishing and praying as leisure-time activities, had in his 83rd year "traveled 19,953 miles by plane and 3,000 miles by automobile, delivered nine major speeches and 21 lesser ones" (*Newsweek*, Aug. 18, 1958). In Germany Chancellor Konrad Adenauer on January 5, 1959, celebrated his 83rd birthday in office, a marvel of energy and elasticity, the secret of which, some think "is the regularity and moderation of his habits and above all the daily walk of almost an hour's duration" (David M. Nichol, *Inquirer*, Jan. 8, 1959). In Ireland, Eamon de Valera on June 17, 1959, at 76, long Prime Minister, was elected President of the Republic. In our own 85th Congress at its start most of the members were in their fifties, but 80 house members and 32 senators were between 60 and 69; 34 and 8 were between 70 and 79, and five house members and 3 senators were over 80. Senator Theodore F. Green of Rhode Island, a veteran of the Spanish-American War, was the oldest at 89. In February, 1959, at 91, he relinquished the chairmanship of the Committee on Foreign Relations, but otherwise continues his active role in the senate. *U. S. News* (Feb. 13, 1959) shows pictures of him playing tennis at 87, dancing at 88, and swimming at 90.

In other vocations, Ethel Barrymore, queen of Broadway, who died in June, 1959, just short of 80, had on her 75th birthday still been hard at work making the motion picture, "Young at Heart." William Walter Heffelfinger, great football All-American, first Yale football coach, who died at 86 in April, 1954, played for nine minutes in a driving snowstorm in a football game in Minneapolis at the age of 65. Maurice Chevalier at 69 was playing an old roué in the movie *Gigi* in 1957, planned a one-man show as a farewell tour thereafter, and subsequently would continue to work on his autobiography. He said, "I am crazy about writing. It is a thing I can do as an old man without

getting out of wind" (*Newsweek*, Oct. 7, 1957). Charles Franklin
Kettering, who years ago helped put America on wheels, at 81
still flew his own plane, and was doing research on "the simple
miracle of photosynthesis" (*Newsweek*, July 21, 1959). The almost legendary Albert Schweitzer is still doing active missionary
work in equatorial Africa at 84. And America's most beloved
poet, Robert Frost at 84 is still an active lecturer and consultant
in poetry for the Library of Congress.

When it comes to evidence that people in the later years
can continue in full mental vigor and rise to marvels of accomplishment, Catholics especially have it before their eyes all the
time. They remember that at the very birth of our country, the
Catholic signer of the Declaration of Independence, Charles
Carroll of Carrollton, was also the one who when he died in
1832 at 95 had been for six years the "Last of the Signers." His
cousin, Archbishop John Carroll, the first bishop of the hierarchy
of the United States, also was active to his death at 80.

Catholics have seen the late Holy Father, Pius XII, promulgate
wonderful encyclicals and letters until his death on October 9,
1958. When the cardinals gathered in Rome from twenty-two
nations to elect a new pope, the average age of the fifty-one
cardinals scheduled to attend the conclave was 75.6. One was
92, eleven in their eighties, eleven between 75 and 79, eight
between 70 and 74. Only five were in their fifties and none was
younger. As we all know, they chose Angelo Cardinal Roncalli,
who was 76, to become the 263rd Holy Father, Pope John XXIII.
At an age when most of us little people would consider ourselves
through, Pope John undertook the biggest job on earth and has
been doing it with a brilliance and energy that is the admiration
of the whole world. The trust the Church has traditionally placed
in episcopal sexagenarians and older should remove at least for
Catholics the fear or the excuse that after 65 they are too old to
learn or to do.

Science is accumulating more and more evidence that a mind if
as it grows older it keeps doing what it is made to do — think,

reason, remember — can stay fit indefinitely. Dr. Shock in *Trends in Gerontology* concludes, "The proverb 'Old dogs cannot learn new tricks' is not in accord with research findings on the learning capacity of older people" (p. 81). Dr. Maurice E. Linden, in "The Challenge of the Geriatric Patient," wrote: "Out of 2,607 scientists it is found that most made their major contribution between the ages of 30 and 70. It is not unimportant that 20 of these savants realized their major achievement after the age of 70" (p. 5). Dr. Martin Gumpert maintains,

> After the critical age between fifty and sixty has been passed, there often seems to be a new flowering of gifts and talents, colored by all the splendor of the setting sun. . . . Great longevity demands new, almost life-long education (quoted in Arthur, *op. cit.*, p. 193).

Since, however, there is usually some fire where there is a lot of smoke, it is well to consider what scientific evidence indicates as to the mental slowing up in the later years. Professor Drake's summary on this question is, "It must be concluded that there is some slowing down of the mental processes as individuals become older" (*op. cit.*, p. 307). Dr. Stieglitz holds that while many functions do slow up they do so very slowly. This holds specifically for that of learning. He states:

> As measured by a group at Columbia University, the rate of learning reaches its peak at age 22. At age 80 it is about the same as at 12 (*U. S. News*, Feb. 14, 1958).

In other words, the ten-year jump in basic learning power from 12 to 22 recedes so gradually that it takes sixty years to retrogress to the learning ability we had at twelve. And it will be noted that at twelve boys and girls, especially bright ones, are thought to enjoy very good years for learning. Dr. Stieglitz adds,

> The false concept that "you can't teach an old dog new tricks" has done a great deal of harm. First of all, it is false, and secondly, it's a wonderful alibi for indolence.

The happy fact seems to be that of all of our capacities our mental ones, if kept in use, last longest. Dr. Linden wrote,

. . . prime attainment in vision is reached around 25 to 30; in hearing it has already been passed in the early 20s. Muscular-reaction time has reached its peak around age 17; vocabulary and ability to define words continue to increase even past 60 (*Parade*, Dec. 12, 1954).

As a matter of fact an increasing number of recent researches suggest that for practical purpose most minds, if kept in vigorous use, do not reach their prime until fifty and even after that do not necessarily decline. Dr. Wilma T. Donahue, University of Michigan gerontologist, summarizes recent studies as follows:

> Mental functions can be maintained at maximum performance, or even increased, for many years. At 70, most people are as mentally capable as they were at 50. Even at 80, one's intellect is often roughly equivalent to what it was in his 20's.

This encouraging statement by an authority is quoted in an article entitled "The Older the Smarter: Your brain improves with age and use" (by Jack Harrison Pollack, *Catholic Digest*, Apr., 1959). Persons who had taken intelligence tests thirty years ago and were now retested show "an actual gain in their intelligence scores," reports *U. S. News* (Dec. 29, 1958), so that the conclusion seems warranted "that lazy thinking — failure to use the brain regularly — is probably as great a threat to mental powers as aging."

Evidence is accumulating that such specific mental abilities as memory and the ability to learn do not decline any more than does general intelligence. Dr. Irving Lorge of Columbia Teachers College "found that people up to 70 could learn Russian and shorthand as easily as their younger classmates." Despite the popular belief, even the memory does not appreciably deteriorate in people who concentrate on what they are doing and what they should remember. Sometimes older people seem to be more forgetful, according to Psychologist Harold E. Jones of the University of California, "because they have so much to forget." As we grow older we store more and more items in our memory, and the more there are, like volumes in a library, the harder they are to find.

In short, observation and researches indicate that most people can think virtually as well at 70 as at 20, can remember what they concentrate on, and can learn more of the old and unquestionably can also start learning something brand new. What slowing up there might be seems to be adequately compensated for by the experience and resourcefulness years of intellectual efforts have provided. The mind does not seem to wear out — it merely rusts away if it isn't used. For a happy and beneficent old age we must keep using our minds — to increase our store of old knowledge and probably also to open up something new. Dr. Shock finds that "everyone, regardless of age, gains satisfaction from acquiring new skills" and urges those in the later years to keep some of the same curiosity which characterizes the young" (*Trends in Gerontology*, p. 81).

It seems to be a general principle of nature that when it provides a capacity it wants it to be used. If in the later years we can think and learn, then, to keep from deteriorating, we must do it. The problem for continued learning in the later years is finding the motivation. Lillien J. Martin wrote:

> Work with the old leads us to believe that the large majority of cases of slowing down in all fields of activity is due to want of motivation or incentive. The person who does not find life worth living will naturally slump in thought and action. To counter this mental apathy by mental stimulation is the aim in salvaging old age.[1]

Everybody seems to agree that in the later years, "The major problem," as Dr. Shock puts it, "is that of motivation." When young, the natural curiosity for asking questions, for learning, is powerfully encouraged by the prodding of parents, by the desire to impress classmates and sweethearts, and most of all by the economic drive for position and promotion.

Even the most devoted workers, the seemingly most selfless teachers, doctors, scientists often unconsciously owe a greater share of their motivation to economic urgency than they realize. Many a university instructor who turns out monograph after

---

[1] Quoted in Clare de Cruchy, *Creative Old Age*, Old Age Counseling Center, San Francisco, 1946, p. 41.

monograph, himself convinced he is doing it for the pure love of scholarship, finds that pure love strangely becoming tepid after his promotion to the full professorship — and cold upon retirement! When retirement removes the motivation for keeping our vocational efficiency primed, we may find ourselves alarmingly without any motivation at all, a prey to vegetation!

This danger should be recognized and counteracted by every religious and cultural means at our disposal. One retired professor, signing himself Josiah Partridge, in "The Man Called 'Ex,'" describes the danger of losing motivation when he broke "out of the Ivory Tower after forty years." He had had long range projects on "Studies in the Art of Translation." Upon retirement, going to Florida he found many people just "sitting on benches," or "playing checkers," or idly talking, and many more just sitting, giving "the impression of contented inertia." He confesses how fortunate he was in this setting to find four men each of whom "was enthusiastic about something" — a biologist, a clergyman, a general practitioner, and a librarian, all retired. He writes,

> They were better table companions because each one had spent the forenoon working at a definite task, so that they had something to relax from.

One was continuing his biological researches, two were writing memoirs, one was "preparing a report on the use of microfilms in libraries," and he himself, stimulated by their intellectual interests, continued his translation studies.

These gentlemen had ideal interests and enthusiasms for the later years. People in teaching, like Partridge, and perhaps also in law, politics, or any of the more challenging occupations, probably often during the press of their prime, hope, when in the later years a letup comes, to do some of the background studying for which they feel the need but lack the time. What professional person has time to keep up as he should with relevant publications! Early in life I realized that, since life was too short to read all good books, even all English classics,

I better ration myself to two or three masterpieces of the greatest authors and to only one of the secondary ones.

Thereafter, often when lecturing on an author, partly to inculcate a similar practice in my students, I would confess that the only book of his I had read was so and so and probably would not get the chance to read another of his until after my retirement! One day talking in this wise, it hit me like a lightning bolt that in fact my unconscious motive for trying to read all the classics systematically was to draw upon them for my teaching, that once retired, my real motive for such reading would be gone! This realization shattered me considerably. Just when I would have the time for such methodical reading, when in fact it might be most beneficial and necessary for my personality during senescence, the practical motivation would have vanished!

How many of us who work on some project with dead earnestness, ostensibly for the good of the cause, unconsciously do it for proficiency in our profession and promotion! Then, when in the later years we finally have adequate time for our project, we feel no use for it any more. That is the tragedy of it. In the retired later years, just when a passion for some project is a mental lifesaver, the passion and the motivation too often die together. It is sadly true that most of the world's accomplishments are due to someone's need for making a living!

For that reason, even in the later years, when a continuing interest in something is so important, the surest way of retaining it is its promise of income! In old age it is too often true for all but the few endowed with a high idealism or spiritualism what Belloc expressed in an ironic couplet:

> I'm tired of love, I'm even tired of rhyme,
> But money gives me pleasure all the time!

Yet somehow for the all-important job of keeping our minds fit, we should in the later years retain or develop some interest, project, or passion, whether it lines our pockets, enlarges our fame, or merely occupies our minds.

The realization that continued use of our mind, improving an old subject or learning a new, is the greatest possible blessing; for our own physical, mental, and even spiritual health can be enough motivation. After my retirement, for example, even though I can no longer use in the classroom what I get out of any classic, it will make me much more interesting to myself and to others if I nevertheless continue with my project of reading systematically the world's greatest books.

What is best suited for any particular individual depends of course on his personal capacity, background, and tastes. The degree of schooling of those reaching the later years varies widely. According to Dr. Shock, "More than one-fifth of those over 65 had less than five years of formal schooling, . . . actually 7 per cent have had none. In 1950, half of the people aged 65 and over had received less than 8.2 years of formal education, whereas half of those 25–29 had received at least 12.1 years of schooling" (*Trends in Gerontology*, p. 82). Such variant degrees of formal education also reflect levels of native capacity. But whatever our degree of education or talent we should all our lives, but especially in the later years, make sure to keep our mind fit. This is not only a material requirement but also a spiritual one. In the parable, the Lord called the servant who had buried his one talent wicked and slothful, and ordered him cast "out into exterior darkness" (Mt. 25:30).

Certainly, as long as the eyes permit, every one in the later years ought to keep on reading. The lowliest ones should at least read the daily paper and a religious weekly. Those with a little more talent should read some news weeklies, and we who are Catholic should by all means read regularly some of the Catholic magazines. Happily we have a wide choice of them, learned and popular. In the secular range there are also increasingly better ones devoted specifically to the later years, one or the other of which may prove interesting even to oldsters not much accustomed to reading.[2]

---

[2] More and more magazines for those 65 and over are being founded: three before me are *Modern Maturity* (310 E. Grand Avenue, Ojai, Calif.); *Retirement Life* (1625 Connecticut Ave., Washington 9, D. C.); *The 65*

In addition to newspapers and magazines, everybody ought to read some books. Everywhere there are libraries with books for every taste and talent. Spiritual books — the Bible, lives of the saints, apologetics; vocational books, how-to-do books; trade and business books; and literary books — travel, history, fiction, poetry. Whatever is worthwhile requires some will and effort: we usually get the most out of precisely those books which challenge our concentration. If anyone unhappily failed earlier in life to acquire the habit of reading books — at least a few a year — he should consider the later years the last chance to start. His reward will be manifold.

In our time, there are other rich channels for mental cultivation — motion pictures, radio, and television. We should consciously try to elevate our tastes and hear and witness programs our common sense tells us are somewhat more elevated in appeal than mere soap opera. In any case, it is better to watch or hear some program than just to sit and daydream.

Some games are useful for keeping the mind fit. One thinks of chess, checkers, and bridge. Most hobbies are good mind polishers. Almost any keen interest in a wholesome activity or project, an interest that in "The Man Called 'Ex'" is referred to as "being enthusiastic about something," tends to keep our minds fit and alert. An Office of Education Bulletin, *Education for a Long and Useful Life* (No. 6, Reprint, 1954) affirms:

> Studies among the aged invariably show, other elements being equal, that those with deep, and varied interests are happier than those with only a few superficial ones. Adults of any educational level can develop interests, although those of higher educational levels are able to acquire broad interests more easily (p. 21).

Skills like square dancing, ceramics, painting, and music contribute wonderfully to keep our minds fit — and happy — in the later years.

The very wisest thing anyone approaching retirement or in it

Magazine (204 W. Broad St., Quakertown, Pa.). These are monthiles and popular magazines. The chief American learned ones are *Geriatrics*, *Journal of Gerontology*, and *Journal of the American Geriatrics Society*.

can do to keep his mind fit and his quota of like-minded friends full is to enroll in whatever suitable adult courses church, lodge, or community offer. Adult education is happily growing everywhere. It is finally being recognized that the mind was made not only to learn up to twenty-one but to the very end. The mind that can learn must learn if it is expected to function well, and not to rust into senility.

The old proverb, *Mens sana in corpore sano* — "A sound mind in a healthy body," is also true in reverse: A sound mind tends to keep the body healthy. Both complement each other. Of the two, the sound mind is the more important. We owe it to ourselves, our relatives, our community, and God to do what we can to keep our mind fit — that is to keep thinking, memorizing, learning with it just as long as we can.

CHAPTER VIII

Considering the Problem of Senility

EVEN if we discount optimistic findings on the learning ability of people over 65, they do indisputably establish that most of us can retain most of our mental powers into the seventies and not abnormally even into the eighties. Most of us can continue to learn provided we keep on learning. Using our mind won't wear it out, but not using it will rust it out. Unfortunately, however, whether through disuse, abuse, or ailment, not all minds can in the later years resist the erosions of senile infirmity.

The mind is our noblest faculty; the one that elevates us above the beasts and can make us like unto either the angels or the demons. One could wish that the Creator had seen fit to spare man the possible humiliation of being able to "lose his mind." But He has not. And it is logical that if a man can sinfully lose his soul to the devil after death, he can also suffer impairment of his mind before. In this as in other matters, God's will be done — even the impairment of one's mind can conceivably, in that it lessens our responsibility, promote our salvation.

Mental illness is a growing American affliction. According to the U. S. Public Health Service it is our top health problem. According to the Public Affairs Pamphlet, "When Mental Illness Strikes Your Family" (Kathleen Doyle, No. 172, July, 1956), it affects more people than cancer, polio, and heart ailments combined and requisitions nearly half of all the hospital beds in the country. It is calculated that one in twenty will sometime in his life be so ill mentally as to need hospitalization, and that

another one in twenty will suffer severe emotional maladjust-
ment. In 1953 the American Medical Association in a survey of
5443 hospitals reported 583,826 mental patients in them.

A relatively large proportion of the mental patients in hospitals
and elsewhere, as is to be expected, are in their later years. Of
the total of 583,826 mental patients in the hospitals, 129,488 were
65 and over, amounting to 22.2 per cent. In 1950, when those
65 and over were 8 per cent of the population, they constituted
25 per cent of the patients of mental hospitals. The increase in
the admission rate to hospitals for the mentally ill of elderly
people, especially those from cities and towns, is considered one
of the most serious manifestations of ill health among the aged.
During the past half century the number and percentage of aged
admitted to mental hospitals has increased rapidly.

However, as Professor Drake points out, "A great deal of this
increase may reflect social-cultural conditions" (*op. cit.*, p. 308).
There are now more and better hospitals for the mentally ill
than formerly. Since there is now less social stigma attached to
mental illness, families are less hesitant to commit an elderly
relative to one. Sometimes committing a relative to a mental
hospital seems an easy way out of an unpleasant situation. One
report finds as follows:

> Whenever an aged patient cannot care for himself and he has
> no one to care for him, he eventually goes to the state hospital,
> although many of the aged presently admitted for care in a mental
> hospital show nothing more important than memory impairment,
> confusion, and physical infirmity. It seems evident that many
> who come to the mental hospital come primarily for sociologic
> reasons.[1]

The point for us seems to be that while the aged who are
afflicted with cerebral arteriosclerosis or senile dementia are a
great, sometimes unwarranted strain on the hospitals of the
country, their numbers do not suggest that most older people
will develop these mental impairments. In 1950, for example,
of the 12,269,537 persons 65 and over, only 385,419 were in

---

[1] Quoted from Dorothy C. Tompkins, *The Senile Age Problem in the
United States*, University of California, Berkeley, Jan., 1955, p. 19.

institutions, and fewer than half of these, only 141,346, were in mental hospitals. Of these, 6850 were in private, 2674 in federal, and 131,822 in state and local hospitals. More than a third, 54,732, were over 75 (see Tompkins, *op. cit.*, p. 65). On the basis of these figures, 98–99 per cent of us will not suffer serious mental breakdowns. Dr. Maurice E. Linden, Director, Division of Mental Health, Philadelphia, in "Personality Changes in the Elderly Person," writes,

> The actual number of older persons who develop psychological disturbances of such magnitude as to require institutionalization is in the neighborhood of 5% to 7% in the 65-and-older category.

Even though five to seven per cent of fifteen million is a number greater than hospitals now can accommodate, it is not so many as to deprive us of the reasonable hope that if we take proper precautions we may be spared the pathetic trials of serious mental disorders.

The causes and conditions of psychoses, usually called insanity in the old days, are at best complicated and problematic. Oldsters seem happily to be spared the more sensational types that often make the headlines in crime news. Julietta K. Arthur writes that "the cases of schizophrenia, manic-depressive psychoses, general paresis, or alcoholic psychoses — rarely appear after sixty-five" (*op. cit.*, p. 305). Old-age psychoses are seldom lurid or violent. Dorothy C. Tompkins defines the senile as

> aged persons who have a marked loss of memory, are childish, mildly irritable, restless at night, careless in toilet habits, bedridden by infirmities of old age, and who become troublesome nursing problems because of personal habits (*op. cit.*, p. 17).

Three types of mental impairment are peculiar to aging. The first is involutional psychosis or melancholia. It is sometimes called middle-age depression. It has some association with the change of life, and occurs in women between 40 and 55 and in men between 55 and 65. It is not organic, however, but emotional. It affects women more than men. It is characterized by depressions, delusions, personality changes, and accounts for some 3 per cent to 4 per cent of the admissions to mental hospitals. It

seems to be an extreme manifestation of the difficulty we all
have to a greater or lesser degree of accepting the fact of growing
old. If we have not conditioned ourselves for the later years
their early signals can be distressing: gray hair, change of vision,
impaired hearing, sexual decline. Dr. Boas writes: "The mere
awareness of waning bodily strength comes as a shocking discovery. . . . In women, the loss of good looks, the appearance
of wrinkles and gray hair, the development of a pendulous
abdomen . . . all forcefully call attention to the passing years"
(*op. cit.*, p 239).

Some sense of depression is likely to be suffered off and on
by everyone at that period of life. In some few, probably those
who all along clung most to youth and did not mature with
their years, this precipitates a severe flight from reality, delusions of youth, and mental breakdown. Julietta K. Arthur writes
that not all persons can take the harbingers of old age philosophi-
cally. The realization that most opportunities are gone, that old
age must be faced, "is the stiffest test of mental stability we are
called on to encounter." She continues:

> For a great many, particularly those never able to make easy
> adjustments or adaptations at any time of life, the realization of
> the burdens old age usually brings comes as a serious emotional
> shock. It may result in a mental breakdown, either temporary or
> permanent (*op. cit.*, p. 304).

Surely we are justified in hoping that if from our youth we have
trained ourselves to accept God's will meekly, we will not be
included in the three or four per cent of middle-agers afflicted
with this extreme melancholia. In any case may our firm resolve
to submit to God's will moderate this and any emotional trials
that tend to encompass the best of us, both men and women,
when we experience the so-called change of life.

The type of illness that has its onset somewhat later, at about
65, is cerebral arteriosclerosis, also called arteriosclerotic dementia.
This worries me most personally, not only because it is more
common among men than among women, but because it has
an organic basis. It comes from some real damage of areas of the

brain. While its effects, like that of all psychoses, are emotional, its causes are damaged brain tissues. Where there is such brain damage, from cerebral hemorrhages or thromboses or whatever, obviously our strongest will and most virtuous disposition cannot unaided prevent our acting more or less crazy. This dementia tends to develop paranoid attitudes and delusions of persecution. These delusions often arise suddenly and distressingly impute to those nearest and dearest the intent to cheat and harm them. It is not only an especially mean form of aberration, but one that can even resort to violence. Furthermore, to the usual psychotic symptoms, there will often be added some paralysis. When this dementia strikes us down, our only hope is that our relatives will get us good medical care betimes and stand patiently and long-sufferingly by us.

The third mental illness peculiar to the later years is senile dementia. Unlike arteriosclerosis, it is functional rather than organic — in the mind rather than the brain. It strikes comparatively late, after 75, and more women than men. It is an acute exaggeration of the natural characteristics of aging. It creeps upon its victims, evolves slowly, and is to be feared more and more as one lives into the eighties. It most clearly presents the symptoms popularly associated with senility: forgetfulness, confusion, mental wandering, untidiness, and even loss of moral judgment. If not arrested, it gets worse and worse until there is complete childishness or worse.

The best one can say regarding this senile dementia is that it is not inevitable or universal in old age, not even extreme old age. Statistically, most of us will escape it. The more we have all our lives kept our emotions and appetites in line with right reason and the will of God, the more likely we are to be spared this mental ravage in our last years.

This is happily the likelihood for all three types of senile psychoses. Unfortunately however no one can have absolute security. Anyone might suffer some brain damage which could lead to cerebral arteriosclerosis. Furthermore, while mental illness is not inherited, a predisposition to it may be. Some individuals do inherit a more delicate mental balance, more easily provoked to a breakdown. Happily they can wisely by taking special care to keep their emotions controlled, their griefs, angers, hates restrained, counteract their inherited predisposition fairly well. Dr. George S. Stevenson, Consultant, National Association of Mental Health, says, "One always has the opportunity of deflecting hereditary tendencies by careful control of environment" (see Arthur, *op. cit.*, p. 305).

But unfortunately, for anyone, with or without any inherited weakness, who has or has not been sensible and moderate all his life, there is still the possibility of an adversity so great or a shock so sudden that it might snap the mind, even if only temporarily. In *Titus Andronicus*, a grandsire rightly holds that "Extremity of griefs would make men mad." In the contemplation of mental disorders, the best of us feel uneasy. Self-consciously we echo Johannes Baptista Mantuanus, when he said in his Eclogues, "It is a common calamity: we are all mad at some time or other." Those of us especially who are guilty of any intellectual vanity will uneasily recall Seneca's saying in his "Tranquility of the Mind" that "There is no genius without some touch of madness." Aristotle wrote, "No excellent soul is exempt from a mixture of madness"; and the great Catholic poet Dryden asserted that, "Great wits are sure to madness close allied, / And thin partitions do their bounds divide."

Perhaps in a disturbed moment, some of us have even felt like exclaiming with Charles Baudelaire, the translator of Edgar Allan Poe: "Today I had a strange warning. I felt the wing of insanity brush my mind." If we did, we might be relieved to have the experts tell us that while we can still reflect on our own sanity or lack of it, our mind is probably quite sound!

To those who are entitled to a relatively calm conscience as they approach the later years, one may proclaim as a soothing probability that a clear conscience is in itself a reasonable insurance against mental disorders. Only a few hundred years ago, insanity was considered more of a crime than a disease. Happily Christianized society no longer considers madness a sin nor treats madmen as criminals. Senile dementia or arteriosclerotic dementia are not sins. Nevertheless, if not in the narrow yet in the wider sense, sin is more often than not a major cause. Vices of intemperance and immorality obviously tend to damage the brain and the mind. But also sin in the still wider sense: selfishness, willfulness, unreasonableness, disregard of the rights and feelings of others, violent passions — jealousy, anger, hatred, even uncontrolled grief — these things are hard on the mind. People who are proud and vain, who cannot brook opposition or accept even minor failures, who are always sorry for themselves and seldom for others, who, in short, have not learned to put God's will above their own, such persons will in the later years suffer more than ordinary mental strain. People, also, who have evaded the responsibility of making up their minds, who have wavered indecisively where a weighing of the facts was necessary to make a decision possible and necessary, such people, too, may break down mentally when finally in the later years decisions are forced upon them.

In "Personality Changes in the Elderly Person" (p. 10). Dr. Linden writes:

> Many of the people who in later life fall victim to the tribulations of aging demonstrate personality patterns composed of egocentric drives and self-directed pleasure strivings that can be classified in the generic category, narcissism.

This may be interpreted to mean that people who are so much in love with themselves that they do not properly love God and their neighbors tend to suffer mentally when they see their body deteriorating. People who have all their lives tried to act acceptable in the sight of God, who accepted not only His law but also His will, who loved their neighbors as themselves, stand a good chance of being spared the tragedy of senile dementia. Yet there are just enough cases of fine and sensible people who nevertheless suffer it to make all of us aware of the necessity of trusting more in God than our own merits to keep us sane.

It is not established how effectively if at all we ourselves can prevent inroads on our own mental health. Lay persons tend to feel that if a person were to make up his mind to be sensible, resolutely in small things and big, he could in all but a few cases of organic damage keep his mind fit. They seem to be supported by Dr. William B. Terhune, of the Yale Medical School, Medical Director of The Silver Hill Foundation for Treatment of the Psychoneuroses. In his pamphlet, *Harvest Years* (Mar. 10, 1954), under "Keep Mentally Fit," he writes that many people

> are handicapped by neurotic tendencies which they have picked up with the years — first they gave in to little escape reactions, and other defense mechanisms followed. Neurotic attitudes are the greatest handicaps of older people. They use their troubles as an excuse for not making the effort. The neuroses of old people are unnecessary.

For ourselves personally, it is well to demand of ourselves what Dr. Terhune suggests. For others, we might wisely make charitable concessions. For both ourselves and others we can fearfully realize that once the mind has really become sick a person can himself no longer recognize the symptoms nor resist unaided the impairment. Perhaps it is only those endowed with minds strong enough to resist final impairment who all along had the capacity to control and check all neurotic tendencies.

Certainly the greatest and most distressing trial of those nearest a psychotic relative is that twilight stage when the patient's actions seem increasingly unreasonable, willful, stubborn, "abnormal," but are not yet recognized for what they are — symptoms of a creeping psychosis. It is a moral as well as a social trial, this stage before we realize that our relative's behavior is not ingratitude or sheer orneriness but a mental sickness, over which he has no control any more, which only expert medicine and psychiatry can moderate or cure.

Certain it is that at such a point the patient himself will not recognize his psychosis; in fact he can be recognized as a mental patient by his acting as if only he were normal and sensible and everyone else wrong or insane. From this condition, all of us pray our Lord to spare us.

When we reach that stage we can no longer help ourselves

unaided. Only others can guide us to improvement. But since all of us as we move toward and reach the later years may be called upon to recognize mental impairments in others — perhaps near and dear to us, we should early be alerted to a few hints and helps.

Mental illness fortunately gives warnings; it does not come overnight. It is important to spot these warnings and to recognize psychosis for what it is when it does strike. There are all degrees and kinds of mental disorders. Nor are the lines between the characteristics of normal aging and of psychotic deviation constant or clear. Besides there is every social and moral reason for not imputing "insanity" to anyone falsely or prematurely. Nevertheless, if a person clearly starts offending against common sense, violates the social norms, acts "queer" in any way, his relatives should take a serious if discreet view of the matter. They should not expect the offender to improve under his own power. Most of the ailments of the later years, especially the mental ones are progressive, and unless something is done they get worse rather than better. Relatives should therefore not let the idea of disgrace move them to wishful hoping and concealment, but should immediately seek the best medical aid that is practical.

Some of the warning signs of such disorders in a person are fits of alternating misery and joy, irritableness and outbursts of rage, indecision, refusal to carry out what is obviously the right course, stupid spending or miserly hoarding, delusions of persecutions, complaining of ills doctors cannot find, listlessness and sleeplessness, feverish and impetuous talking, personal untidiness, unwarranted anxieties and "imagining things." If we can recognize any of these in ourselves, and can both admit and check them, we are still safely normal. If we have several of them but cannot recognize them and will not admit them, then it is up to our relatives to get us psychiatric care immediately.

Increasingly, science can promise mental patients palliation or relief. In "A New Way to Help Old People with Problems," Dr. Linden writes,

One of the best pieces of news in medicine today is that the common signs of mental decline in older people can be lessened or even stopped in eight out of 10 cases. . . . People do get old, body and mind do slow up. But what you and I have heard referred to as "senility" — memory loss, grouchiness, fear, periods of melancholy — is largely unnecessary (pamphlet, Department of Public Health, Philadelphia, n.d.).

An increasing number of promising treatments is possible. Regarding "memory loss," for example, *U.S. News* (Aug. 1, 1958) reported that "Injections of certain nucleic acids — substances found in protein — help clear up the inability to remember things that occurs in aged persons." In "When Mental Illness Strikes Your Family," Kathleen Doyle lists and briefly describes such treatments and psychotherapies: psychoanalysis, narcosynthesis (the use of "truth serums," pentothal or sodium amytal), group psychotherapy, occupational therapy, hydrotherapy (continuous bath, or wet pack, or needle shower), shock therapy, and lobotomy. The most publicized methods in recent years have been the shock therapies: insulin shock and electroshock. Dr. Boas, though thinking that the treatment with electric shock is used far too freely, nevertheless explains: "It is astonishing how well most old persons, even those with hypertensions or arteriosclerosis, tolerate shock therapy" (*op. cit.*, p. 244). Lobotomy is the last resort of the therapies — a surgical operation severing "some of the fibers connecting the front lobes of the brain with the thalamus or emotional center of the brain" (Doyle, *op. cit.*, p. 24). While this may bring on an untoward change of personality and apathy in a patient, it can at least relieve mental suffering in the incurably ill.

Dr. Linden in his pamphlet on "A New Way to Help Old People with Problems" (Department of Health, Philadelphia), gives a splendid table of psychotic symptoms in the order of their relievability by group therapy. These symptoms can serve as a valuable check list for ourselves, if we are still mentally well, in trying to stay well. If we are already ill, they can help our relatives recognize our condition and provide the psychiatric help, which at that point we urgently need but can no longer realize the need ourselves.

In the first category Dr. Linden lists the symptoms for which there is the greatest likelihood of relief. *Good results may be expected when:*

(1) The patient forgets current events, but remembers remote events.
(2) His personality changes from, say, happiness to melancholy, or neatness to slovenliness.
(3) He appears preoccupied or becomes absent-minded.
(4) He says he feels useless, shows little interest in friends, isolates himself or says he feels excluded.
(5) He becomes very talkative or very withdrawn.
(6) He shows little interest in food (although this may be entirely physical).
(7) He says he is frightened and cannot sleep.

In the second category, of more serious symptoms, *fair results may be expected when:*

(1) The patient is hostile, unfriendly and cantankerous.
(2) He displays increased interest in children and displays childish behavior.
(3) He indulges in fantasies and begins to believe that such daydreams are real.
(4) He is occasionally incoherent and his thoughts are garbled.
(5) He hoards sundry items — mostly useless — believing that they will "come in handy someday."
(6) He is excessively restless or excessively overactive.

In the third category, *generally only poor results may be expected when:*

(1) The patient is only sporadically able to recognize relatives and friends.
(2) He tends to wander about and get lost.
(3) He complains constantly of aches and pains and feels that he is being persecuted.
(4) He believes he is being robbed or "put upon" constantly.

Group therapy is of course only one of several therapies. Where it fails or only partially succeeds, other therapies, such as chemotherapy, shock therapy, or lobotomy, which are more radical, may succeed.

When we ourselves are struck down with arteriosclerotic or with senile dementia responsibility largely passes from us to our relatives and to the community. For we then can no longer know our duty to ourselves or others. But when it is our relative who suffers this misfortune, ours is the burden and the responsibility for his welfare here and hereafter. Probably his awareness and suffering will be less than ours. That reflection may somewhat lighten our distress at witnessing a loved one's tragic senility.

To fulfill our reponsibility properly toward the senile demented requires not only good will but much knowledge and wisdom. Since this predicament fortunately strikes only a small percentage of people in the later years, it would carry us too far to attempt detailed directions. When that burden devolves upon us, we should confer with the family doctor and the pastor. We should directly seek information from the nearest mental hygiene clinic, state department of mental health, or state mental health society.[2] We will probably have to engage a qualified psychiatrist, who cannot only treat the patient but advise us as to what we should do and how we should treat our dear afflicted one. With his help we can settle the important matter of hospitalization.[3]

If like Thomas Gray's tenderhearted folks, we incline to suffer more "for another's pain" than for our own, our burden will be doubly heavy. But in the most despairing moments we can lift up our hearts in grateful thanksgiving to God that He kept our own mind sound enough to be able to help our stricken relative. And we should pray every day for the gift of a sound mind to our last days!

---

[2] Mental health clinics are available in some 1150 areas of the United States. For information about the nearest one, you can write to The National Association for Mental Health, 10 Columbus Circle, New York 19.

[3] For an informal "first aid" of information in the event of a mental breakdown in our family, I strongly recommend Kathleen Doyle's *When Mental Illness Strikes Your Family*, Public Affairs Pamphlet No. 172, July, 1956 (22 East 38th St., New York 16, 25 cents).

CHAPTER IX

Keeping Financially Fit

MOST important after health seems to be financial security. When old people are questioned, they first of all want health and after that enough money to be a burden to no one. Dr. Steincrohn writes, "The fear of financial insecurity is third in magnitude only to the fear of loss of health and the fear of death" (*op. cit.*, p. 227). In this world, however pleasant it would be to take our Lord's words literally, ". . . be not solicitous for your life, what you shall eat, nor for your body, what you shall put on" (Mt. 6:25), the fact remains we must be concerned about keeping economically fit. The birds of the air "neither sow, nor do they reap," and the heavenly Father provides for them — except when a frost or a drought decimates them! We human beings, however, as the same heavenly Father in anger told Adam, shall only "with labour and toil" all the days of our life wring from the earth the bread we eat (Gen. 3:17). Whatever the sparrows do, we it is certain must toil for our keep and be concerned for our means of support to the very end, nay, even for the very considerable expense attendant upon our burial thereafter.

What may someday be recognized as a revolutionary change affecting the whole structure of our way of life occurred in 1935 when the first Social Security legislation was enacted and since then continually broadened. In the previous 160 years of our national existence, security in one's old age was one's own and one's family's responsibility. In extreme cases the country provided a "poorhouse." All in all, this system of personal responsibility for security in the later years seemed not to work so badly. Recently President Eisenhower reminisced:

> When I was a boy, it was thought we could live our lives on a little piece of ground in the West, and the old folks — grandfather and grandmother — could live in the same home, after their days of hard work were ended. That's the way we took care of ourselves and our older people. Today, through the changes in our industrial system, we as a people have become dependent for old age security more and more upon pensions.

The Wall Street Journal, in "The Pension Society," comments on the President's reflections:

> Today, for better or for worse, we are all joining the pension society. The present generation doesn't privately take care of grandmother; the sons leave that to the State or to the corporate pension (June 9, 1959).

The old family-responsibility system worked so well perhaps because in the good old days far fewer people lived into the sixties and seventies, least of all among the very poor. The few who did live into the later years rather naturally found themselves quite useful in an age of large houses and few conveniences.

In any case the introduction and growth since 1935 of the Old Age Assistance and the Old Age Survivors Insurance represent a radical departure from the traditional American way of life. Whether in the long run the new emphasis on government responsibility for old age security will prove wholesome cannot certainly be foreseen now. It is probable, however, that the progressive income tax, more and more onerous since its inception in 1913, the enormous war and cold-war military expenditures, and the eroding inflation have made something like the Social Security program necessary.

What seems certain to me is that the assurance in the later years of monthly federal checks, given as a pension, not as a charity, if it will not socialize our whole American way of life, will at least change the whole American attitude toward leisure and retirement. Until lately, the American custom, somewhat unique and dating to colonial days, of considering doing nothing a sin, of expecting even the wealthy not to idle, has given old people, even when legitimately retired or pensioned, a shelved, frustrated, and guilty feeling.

But within a few decades, human nature ever adjusting more easily to leisure than to labor, the millions receiving government pensions will feel proud rather than ashamed of their leisure. In pagan societies leisure was ever a mark of pride; only Christianity stamped labor with glory and put a taint of laziness on leisure. In America the Christian ideal of work took hold with a unique compulsiveness and is the cornerstone of America's astounding material wealth. Some may say that with Americans the virtue of work has been carried to excess, but certain it is that human nature being what it is this passion for work can with perilous ease be converted into a love of *dolce far niente*. Pension recipients will also accommodate themselves rather easily to revising their standard of living downward to a level consistent with the pension check, provided this can be stretched to cover the minimal needs and that many others are on their level. They will form their own groups on the basis of pension income. Anyone who knows Europe is familiar with ever present sets of rather contented pensioners.

At any rate the present social security system guarantees all Americans in their later years a minimum monthly income — enough surely for the "daily bread" implored in the Lord's Prayer. Under the Social Security Act of 1935, the government provides Old Age Insurance, which is treated as a pension, and also sponsors in co-operation with state governments, Old Age Assistance, which is a charity. In the Old Age Assistance program the Federal Government assists any state with nearly two thirds of any amount which a state allots to a destitute person 65 and over up to a combined total of $65 a month. During the early years of the Old Age Insurance program, it was found that many needy oldsters were not covered by that program at all or were not entitled to substantial payments. As an effective way to reach the needy aged quickly, the Federal Government made available to the states tempting sums which they must at least partially match in order to get.

This whole program has been wisely calculated to help the very poor everywhere, and to induce especially the underdeveloped states to give some assistance to their aged poor. By September, 1938, all states had qualified, and now Alaska, Hawaii, Puerto Rico, and the Virgin Islands are included too. Congress has periodically liberalized the measure in amounts and in application. By October, 1958, it raised the allowed maximum from $55 a month to $65, offered to pay $41.50 of this amount, requiring the state to pay only $23.50. It also allowed the calculation to be based on the state's average recipients rather than on each individual recipient. The federal Old Age Assistance money is a bonanza for the states. Some of the more advanced and richer states, which in any case felt bound in charity to help their needy aged, double or triple the Federal Government's share. In Pennsylvania, for example, an individual can get as much as $105 a month from this program. It is administered not by a federal agency but by a State Welfare Agency — in Pennsylvania, for example, by the State Department of Public Welfare.

Old Age Assistance is really a clever and admirable program for discovering and helping old folks in need. Its local administration enables assessment of real need; its being in the nature of a charity rather than a pension tends to confine it to those really without means. But for that reason it is of little help to the genteel poor, who have some property but no income. It is of maximum help to those classes who seldom save and who live from hand to mouth. It does assure them of some income in their old days, enough probably to make it possible for someone in their own relationship or circle to give them room and board.

From the beginning it was planned that as Old Age Insurance covered more people for large amounts, the Old Age Assistance program would wither away to a small emergency level. So far, however, it has grown rather than declined. Its administration is big business; it involves determining the eligibility and making periodic payments to some 2.6 million persons each year, and requires a staff of at least 25,000 people. In 1936 there were

786,000 recipients, in 1940 nearly 2 million; by 1950, nearly 2.8 million. By then, 22.5 per cent of all persons 65 and over received old-age assistance. Whether with the increased coverage and higher payments of the old age insurance program (Social Security) since 1959, the old age assistance program will in fact decline is a precarious hope. It offers politicians too tempting a chance to buy popularity with the Federal Government's money. A reduction is in order, however, and should be worked for.

While it is in operation — and in a contracted form it will probably always be needed for a minimum of the unfortunate or improvident — it does assure every destitute American in the later years at least his daily bread. But for American society as such, for the broad mass of fifteen million in their later years and the many more millions looking forward to them, the most important economic factor is the increasing role of the Social Security pension program.

As Governor of New York, Franklin D. Roosevelt in 1931 shrewdly said,

> Our American aged do not want charity, but rather old-age comforts to which they are rightfully entitled by their own thrift and foresight in the form of insurance (see Corson and McConnell, *op. cit.*, p. 187).

With the introduction of the Old Age and Survivor's Insurance in 1935, since then periodically enlarged in coverage, in payments, and in worker and employer contributions, virtually everybody, regardless of status or wealth, is assured during his retirement a substantial government pension. According to the latest liberalization in January, 1959, some 12.7 million persons 65 and over and retired are assured of minimum federal pensions of $33 a month and a maximum of $116, which maximum even without further action of congress will in some years become $127. For a worker and wife the maximum is now $174 and the dollar maximum on family benefits was raised from $200 to $254 a month. One can assume that in a few more years everybody will be considered covered under the pension fund, regardless of how little he paid into it.

There is no doubt that this guarantee as a right, not as a charity, of a substantial pension upon retirement has for all of us changed our outlook on the later years. It will eventually profoundly modify our American way of life and the attitude on work and leisure. As it stands now, surely a man who has saved anything at all, who, for example, has paid off his house, does not need to stand in fear and trembling of destitution if he and his wife are assured of a monthly check, rain or shine, tax free, of some $150. Those who have built up an annuity of their own and are beneficiaries of a company pension or have some income from rent, can with the addition of the federal pension look forward to a mode of life in the later years almost as rich and bountiful as during their working days.

This old age security is a wonderful thing — at the rate in which it is expanding, almost too wonderful! It would be tragic if at some time when most needed it would break down. The old-age survivors insurance trust fund tends to be represented as self-supporting, as operating like insurance annuities. But that fund of $18.7 billion in 1953, of $22.6 billion in 1956, was by 1958 not higher, but lower. This fund is valuable as an ideal condition, but it is essentially an illusion, for the fact is, it cannot provide on an insurance basis the huge pension payments. They come actually from the current contributions of workers and employers. At present each employee contributes 2½ per cent of his pay check up to $4,800 to the "fund," and the employer a matching 2½ per cent. But the "fund" is not increasing, it merely equals the pension payments. The deductions, however, are scheduled to increase and indeed have to. By 1969 they are planned to be 4½ per cent. One can say that the worker now pays more into Social Security than until 1940 he paid in total income tax. In addition the employer pays a considerable levy, which he must add to the price of his products or services.

For the future, one must consider that more and more people will draw this pension and at higher amounts, and that with the life span continuing to lengthen they will draw it for more years.

It is estimated that the old-age and survivors insurance, independently of old-age assistance or of anything else, will by 1980 send checks to 85–91 per cent of the aged population and that "the cost of these benefits will approximate $15 billion on an intermediate cost estimate" (see Corson and McConnell, *op. cit.*, p. 427). At present "If the funds set aside annually as reserves are added to the annual expenditures, the cost of the current social provision for the present and future aged approximates $11.6 billion a year." This figures to 3.5 per cent of our current gross national product; the projected cost for 1980 of both the pension and the other benefits is estimated similarly at from 3 to 4 per cent of the gross national product. Such a percentage is considered quite within America's capacity to provide for the aged.

But the heavy burden, while considered possible, assumes that Congress will not substantially raise the benefits, that the retirement age will not be lowered, and that there will be no depressions. Certainly, in depressed times any hope based on the reserve fund is an illusion. Those working will have to pay the benefits. In bad times not enough may be employed for them to carry this burden, especially if it seems unrealistic. One can infer such a possibility from an article regarding the German social security system by Dr. Franz Josef Wuermeling, German Federal Minister for Family Questions, writing of "Alarming Population Trends." These are that in Germany by 1971 the number of men over 65 and women above 60 will have increased 63 per cent since 1951, or from 5.7 million to 9 million. He concludes:

> In short, these statistics indicate that in the future the active segment of our population may not be able to maintain social benefits. . . . Our social prosperity . . . is threatened by national superannuation, on the one hand, and fewer children on the other (*Bulletin*, Bonn, Oct. 18, 1956).

It is well to reckon with the fact that our own social security system, when our time comes to draw benefits, will pay those benefits from what payroll deductions there are then, not from the money we believed we had paid into a retirement fund. Therefore pensions must be kept at a level which can be sustained in bad as well as boom times.

One of the wisest provisions of the present program is that a pensioner may earn up to $100 a month without losing his pension for that month, or $1,200 a year. It seems to me anything which encourages people to keep on working and earning is an excellent thing for themselves and for society. This additional income will greatly improve the happiness of people in the later years, especially of the finer people, those who rather give to society than merely receive from it. Dr. Harry J. Johnson, president of the Life Extension Foundation, in "How to Retire and be Happy," summarized the results of 4000 questionnaires to the retired employees of eight different companies:

> What struck us most forcibly was that money seemed to be a very important consideration, so far as happiness in retirement goes. We found that 86 per cent of those who claimed to be unhappy, bored, etc., were those with an income of less than $5,000 a year. Only 6 per cent of those with $5,000 or more of income said they were unhappy in retirement (*U. S. News*, Feb. 1, 1957).

As Samuel Butler long ago wrote in *The Way of All Flesh*, "If we feel that we have a competence at our backs, so that we can die warm and quietly in our beds, with no need to worry about expense, we live our lives out to the dregs. . . ."

Again, precisely the nobler of the retired people will be the ones who most want to keep on doing some useful work to supplement their competence. In so doing, they may bring a rich blessing to this country. Much work which cannot be paid for at factory rates is still needed here for more cultural and beautiful living. Our vacant lots, our countrysides, the banks of our brooks and rivers are generally ugly and neglected. Anyone who has seen the well-kept gardens, hedges, yards of Europe, the tended brooks and ponds, realizes that much in this country still needs to be done. Culturally, in thousands of homes and clubs, loving hands are needed to put books and paintings in better order. In our Catholic parishes, clubs, and societies, too, much such work wants doing. Men and women, retired, may find it worthwhile to accept the modest pay for such work in order to keep busy and to supplement their pension checks. I recall the happy arrangement that resulted when a worker, an immigrant, upon retirement was able to supplement his social security pension by becoming librarian for his local Ukrainian lodge. In general, I would advise all pensioners, if at all able, to try to get some useful job for the good of society, of their financial fitness, as well as for their sense of accomplishment.

What is not yet nationally recognized but seems absolutely necessary to me if the country hopes to maintain its social security system is to delay the official retirement age rather than to consider making it even lower than the present 65. In as much as science and environment are making people healthier and longer living all the time, people should also be expected to work more years than was customary when the average life span was only fifty. Yet, the figures show that they are working few years. The U. S. Department of Health Publication, *Aging — A Community Responsibility and Opportunity* (n.d.), reports,

> All told, only about 2 out of 5 men over 65 — 2.6 million — are in the labor force in any one month as compared with 2 out of 3 in 1890. The majority are under 70, and roughly one-fourth have only part-time work.

In 1955, for example, fewer than half the men over 65 and fewer than one sixth of the women worked any time.

Given momentum by the Social Security provisions, compulsory retirement programs effective at 65 in government and industry are spreading. They are however accompanied by considerable misgivings and uneasiness on the part of management and dissatisfaction on the part of most types of workers. Generally those workers who enjoy their work and whose earnings are considerably above any combined retirement payments are unhappy at being stamped "Unusable" on the mere basis of a birthday. If we except the few blessed individuals who have a special project awaiting their retirement, it is the best and also the most useful workers who suffer most financially and psychologically from an early compulsory retirement system.

On the other hand, it is not established that the millions who work at uncongenial jobs, or whose total income after taxes is not so appreciably more than the retirement payments, are also resentful of compulsory retirement. It is more probable that most of them would easily and quickly adjust to a life of ease. Such a life is the line of least resistance for human nature. But it is not the line of most value for the human being himself and for society. One might even say that precisely most of those who eagerly accept retirement at any reasonable pension are the ones for whom it would be best if they continued for some years to be usefully employed.

Socially and morally, it seems a rather frightening prospect to think of fifteen million people idling about from 65 to 80. They would be idle for what used to be one fourth of the average life span. If idleness in youth is considered the devil's workshop, there is no reason for believing that it becomes a gymnasium for saints in the old. In a 1959 Labor Day statement, Cardinal Cushing of Boston reminded us that to each man a different task is given and for him "his work is the chief means of salvation." The more work a man does the more merit he is in a position to garner before God. He called the chronic loafer not only a nuisance but judged by Christian standards "downright immoral." The prelate said pointedly:

> Work is not popular with our generation. The shorter working week, shorter working day, shorter working hours are the cry of the times. . . . Some of the reduction of work is understandable and even desirable, but the repugnance for work, the wish to avoid work at all costs, these are unhealthy, unholy and unfortunate signs of the times (from *The Wanderer*, Sept. 3, 1959).

It would seem socially and morally unwholesome, as it is economically precarious, to encourage retirement earlier than realistic health factors require.

The economic burden if retirement at 65 or earlier becomes universal might indeed become insupportable. Though the present payroll deductions and employer contributions to Social Security are burdensome enough, they do not in fact as yet have to support universal retirement at 65. Though 65 for men and 62 for women are sanctioned by Social Security, the actual average retirement age in 1950 for men was 68.7 and for women 68.0. These ages are far more realistic and practical than the "legal" 65 and 62. The danger and the probability is that the ages sanctioned by Social Security will become the universal rule for retirement in both government and industry. Considerable political and social pressure for universalizing retirement at 65, when federal pensions begin, is observable.

Even under present booming conditions, it would be economically unfortunate, aside from the likely moral harm of enforced idleness in oldsters still able to work, if retirement should become general at 65. Corson and McConnell in *Economic Needs of Older People*, 1956 (p. 428), write:

> . . . if universal retirement at age 65 were to become general, the nation would be deprived of the output of about 3 million workers, amounting to about $11 billion in gross national product. Such a development, Sumner H. Slichter has estimated, "would be ten times as costly as the present [1949] old-age program is today."

On the other hand if the average retirement age were raised, if more able older people could and would continue working, "the total share of the gross national product required to finance benefits, at present levels, might be less than 2 per cent" (instead of the 3.5 per cent, which it was even in 1954).

It would seem wise — indeed to me it seems ultimately necessary — for the federal old-age programs to raise the effective pension age from 65 to 68 or to 70. Dr. Harry J. Johnson said:

> I think that 65-year compulsory-retirement age is just about as out-of-date as a "life expectancy" of 60 years would be nowadays. . . . Seventy would be much more realistic, because men in their late 60s today are really in amazingly good physical condition (Interview, *U. S. News*, Feb. 1, 1957).

But industry cannot be expected to keep the retirement age up to 68 or 70, if the Federal Government retires its own employees at 65 and in its social security program fixes 65 as the customary age for starting pensions. Congress instead of debating a lowering of the retirement age previous to every election should, perhaps someday must, resolutely strive to raise it. A well-run organization is one which makes its resources go a long way. We reflect how the Catholic Church in America would fare, usually conceded to be a well-managed organization, if it retired all its priests, brothers, and nuns at 65 with a pension! In the long run a whole country or a large industry is subject to the same conditions of efficiency.

It is true of course that a reversal of trend from lowering the retirement age to raising it would cause some difficulties. Virtually all reversals, especially those from a line of least resistance to one of greater character and economy, cause initial problems and resistance. But it is safe to predict that within a short time people would stop feeling old at 65 and go on working happily until 68 or 70.

It is obvious that if the general retirement age is elevated as suggested, special account must be taken of those who actually cannot work beyond 65. The social security program, which has found ways and means of helping various types of disabled workers, and widows, and dependents, can we may be sure find adequate ways of channeling retirement benefits to those 65 and over who really cannot work up to the revised higher age. These can well enough be discovered by modern diagnostic and testing methods. There won't be very many, once fashion favors working rather than retiring. If things are done right, it will become the custom for most people to work up to the 68 or 70 age level at which Social Security payments would become automatic. Those who cannot, will be in the minority and as such can be handled all the more generously. Almost certainly most people in the later years — and the finer they are the more certainly so — will be grateful for the opportunity to keep usefully employed a further number of years.

In addition to a policy of raising the normal retirement age from 65 to 68 or 70, both government and industry should probably develop and promote a system of *gradual* retirement. It seems unrealistic, as now, to keep on promoting a man virtually right up to 64, and then a year later retire him as no longer worth a salary! In the universities, for example, a man may well be promoted to full professor in his early sixties and at 65 be retired as superannuated! In many occupations, such incongruities occur.

Surely, barring accident or special illness, the sensible policy would be at a certain age, possibly 65, to start reducing a man's load by graduated stages and his income proportionately. When his prospective pension payments approach his reduced salary he would be retired and probably would want to be. In the cultural and intellectual spheres, it has been proved over and over again that some men in their sixties and seventies and even eighties have made invaluable contributions. But also workers on less exalted levels, in fact in most occupations, should not be considered expendible at 65.

The plans for gradual retirement for workers are being discussed more and more frequently. In "'Gradual Retirement' — Latest Idea for Older Workers" *U.S. News* (Sept. 26, 1958), briefly describes five plans for such gradual retirement and mentions some firms trying them. Reportedly the Federal Government is considering this for its own employees. It seems to me a must program if a majority of people in the later years are to be kept happy and useful a maximum of years. If the psychological hurdle between working today and being retired tomorrow can be overcome, then with the right approach the one between reaching the top today and facing a gradual cutback tomorrow can be overcome too!

Being usefully employed is a blessing of which oldsters should not be deprived prematurely. Working as long as possible is generally good not only for their disposition and their soul but also for their body. And having its vast number of elder citizens work into their later years is obviously a good thing for society. As the number of oldsters grows it may become absolutely necessary. The more people work into the later years, the more can society, including federal and state governments, help those who are ill in their old age or who are in the high seventies or eighties where they really can no longer work. All of us can then feel more happy and secure in the knowledge that those in the later years either can take care of themselves or are well taken care of by society and that we ourselves when our turn comes will enjoy the same benefits.

CHAPTER X

Life as a Couple

GIVEN health and enough wealth for food, clothes, and housing, people of any age have the prerequisites for happiness. But to realize it, unless they are uncommonly spiritually minded, they need what is called love. For most human beings, this seems to be an essential for true contentment. While love or the prospect of it is an urgency in the younger years, it remains a restless need to the very end of our days. Fortunate are those who reach the later years happily married and can walk through them hand in hand.

The blessedness of marriage as an institution becomes most evident when a couple, having survived the turbulent, harassed, impassioned green years, mellows into a lovely "togetherness" in their later years. These become golden years, harvest years — the reward for a sacrament faithfully honored in long years and difficult moments. The man and wife of a golden marriage seem almost visibly to become the two in one flesh which is the sacrament. They eventually almost come to resemble each other. Mrs. Clarence H. Hamilton in *Your Rewarding Years* writes:

> There is a unique kind of happiness ahead for the older husband and wife, if they can spend the final years of their lives together. It will not be a repetition of the honeymoon period, but something far richer and deeper. Like the honeymoon, however, it may be a time of discovering some new things in the personality of the beloved companion (New York: 1955, The Bobbs-Merrill Co., p. 29).

Happily the chances of enjoying many later years together are increasing all the time. A typical couple today has twice the chance of surviving to a golden anniversary than it would have had fifty years ago. In 1944 the Metropolitan Life Insurance Company found that,

> Even at age 65, when the husband is ready for retirement, he may expect to share the next eight and one-half years with his wife if she is of the same age (*Statistical Bulletin*, Feb., 1944).

Although these figures have not been recalculated for 1959, they would be even more favorable now.

Unfortunately, sin and stupidity break up more marriages before 65 than death. The ship of matrimony hits some especially rough seas just before it glides into the calm bay of the sixties. A woman in her late forties experiences the so-called change of life during which she often is not much of a comfort to her husband. He in turn, whose facsimile of a change of life usually does not synchronize with his wife's, may react to her coldness by dangerously casting about for one more fling at romance where he should not. And so many a marriage either breaks up or suffers from mutual recriminations and bitterness that leave indelible wounds. Couples in their middle years, who start having special troubles, should go to a proper counselor. If they can be made to see that their distempers and unusual temptations are only temporary, like the last frenzy of devils being exorcised, they can with good will and prayer endure those few years of trial loyally and morally. If they do, their reward in true contentment in the later years will be uniquely satisfying. Seeing couples who have survived the storms and stresses of a long marriage makes one feel as if all the early years were made to provide the quiet trust and joy in one another of the later years. They recall the lyric of Robert Burns:

> And mony a canty day, John, / We've had wi' ane anither;
> Now we maun totter down, John, / But hand in hand we'll go,
> And sleep thegither at the foot, / John Anderson, my jo.

What, beyond each other, such couples need most for happiness is reasonable health and an adequate income. A minimum will do, but, as for all of us all our lives, the more the better.

For that and other reasons, the husband in most cases should continue in his regular job as long as he can. A job gives not only more income than ordinary pensions but also satisfaction, prestige, and social contacts. When St. Paul wrote, ". . . if any man will not work, neither let him eat" (2 Thess. 3:9), he meant that work is good for us, spiritually and materially. Dr. T. N. Rudd, in *The Nursing of the Elderly Sick* ([Philadelphia: Lippincott, 1944], p. 6) approvingly quotes Celsus, of the first century, A.D.: "While inaction weakens the body, work strengthens it; the former brings premature old age, the latter prolongs youth." We should be slow to assume that we are too old to work. We should also, however, recognize the probability that we are not quite so able at seventy as at forty. That means we should graciously accept some reduction in responsibility, in work load, and in salary.

Unfortunately, present ill-advised trends may enforce our retirement and throw us on Social Security even if we are able and willing to stay on our job. If this unavoidably happens to us, we should accept it in the sense that "God's will be done" and make the best of it. We should immediately look about for any other suitable employment, part time or otherwise, which will supplement our pension and give us something useful to do. A wife can keep busy enough with her housework. A husband's case is different, and however much a wife values her husband she generally does not want him in her way in the house all day long. It is good for his self-respect to have something scheduled to do. I recall a gentleman, who just to get out of his wife's way and to impress his neighbors, would leave daily at nine for a broker's office, watch the tape five hours, and come home at four. But he did feel somewhat guilty about the futility of his activity. If he had done some useful work, even on a volunteer basis, for his parish, or club, or any humanitarian organization his satisfaction would have been genuine and deserved.

It is said that one of the worst depressives of the later years is feeling useless. Mrs. Hamilton wrote that "to keep growing one needs to be related to life in some active way. One needs to be needed" (*op. cit.*, p. 140). The way to be needed and not to feel useless is to volunteer to do a few of the thousands of things that need to be done everywhere but for which there are not always adequate funds. One quotes with approval from Frances Sargent Osgood's poem, "Laborare est Orare,"

> Work — for some good, be it ever so slowly;
> Cherish some flower, be it every so lowly:
> Labor! — all labor is noble and holy!

A boon in the later years is owning one's own home along with some little yard and garden. It is the first and best investment a young couple can make — putting a down payment on a home — and usually a considerable asset in old age. Generally, despite high taxes, living in one's own home is cheaper than paying rent. But it also provides the prestige and satisfaction of ownership — along with the responsibilities. The latter include so much need for puttering around, for repairing and improving and keeping in trim, that even if a man is forced out of every outside employment he can get from this a satisfaction similar to that which his wife gets from keeping house. Nor should one assume that because wives keep complaining about the trials of keeping house that they would be happy without them. In fact their continued activity and interest in keeping house may be one reason why they live some six years longer than men!

Several problems often arise with regard to housing for elderly couples. One is when the house, bought years ago, now suffers from a deteriorated neighborhood. This is something that should have been foreseen years before while the couple was still employed and could have traded it more advantageously for another in a better location. However, if the neighborhood has really become too uncongenial, then rather than fret and fear, it would seem generally best to sell as best one can. Thereupon the most desirable thing to do, if that is at all feasible, is to move in with the family of a son or daughter. An important requisite here is that something like a separate apartment can be developed in the younger family's house. Mrs. Hamilton writes: "Next best to having a home of our own, it seems to me, is living in a foster home or living with our children . . ." (*op. cit.*, p. 148). More emphatically, the novelist Pearl Buck recently blamed much of the juvenile delinquency on the present "tendency to separate the generations." She said the self-imposed isolation of the generations, the breakdown of close family ties, has made the American people a lonely people. She said, "Older people need children around them just as much as the children need the opinions and restraints of adults" (see Philadelphia *Evening Bulletin*, Mar. 12, 1959).

Unfortunately some social welfare agencies tend to suggest that for several generations to live under the same roof, for grandparents, parents, and grandchildren to live in the same house, no matter how roomy, is a social disgrace and a psychological handicap. One publication, for example, entitled, *Housing the Elderly* (Housing and Home Finance Agency, Apr., 1959) regrets that "inadequacy of their incomes and the lack of savings . . . play a part in the determination of some married elderly couples to live with their children." This represents an unsound and materialistic tendency. For two related generations to live under the same roof, far from being a psychic liability, is one of nature's simplest ways to insure for everybody a maximum of normality. It should be, as Pearl Buck implies, acclaimed rather than deplored.

When however an elderly couple moves under the same roof with a son's or daughter's family, certain physical prerequisites must be met in order to insure harmonious coexistence. The older couple, having always been used to its own household, must have its own kitchen. It would require a miracle of saintliness for two wives to manage peaceably in one kitchen. It is really highly desirable, if not necessary, to give the elderly couple the essential advantages and privacy of a separate apartment. Their own kitchen, bathroom, and bedroom would seem to be mandatory. Constructing such an apartment or semiapartment in any house, zoning permitting, is much more economical than paying rent or taxes on two separate houses.

If an elderly couple's own house has become too large with

their children married off, the preferable procedure, too, is to convert it into a duplex. The extra dwelling will provide not only extra income, but if rented wisely, good company. If it can be rented to one of their own children, both parties are doubly fortunate.

If an elderly couple finds it necessary or convenient to rent, and cannot do so in the dwelling of a child or other relative, then it is wise to rent first of all near one's favorite parish, second, near the cluster of one's chief friends and relatives, and third, near shopping and similar facilities. One question that becomes more and more acute is whether a retired couple should pull up stakes and move to Florida or some other warmer state. For some this is undoubtedly wise. But it should not be considered best for everybody nor be done without considerable reflection. People who do not easily make new friends are usually happier in the locality where they spent most of their lives and where their old friends or their married children are. Perhaps a most valid statement is that most elderly couples are happiest when they are within at least easy visiting distance of one or all of their grown children.

In the later years, in all plans involving fixed expenses such as rent, transportation, and scale of living, we must realistically take into account our probable monthly income. Young people, justified in expecting progressive incomes, may assume burdens which might prove disastrous for older people, who must reckon with declining income and buying power and should anticipate serious medical expenses. In the later years, perhaps even more than in youth Micawber's words in *David Copperfield* have validity: "Annual income twenty pounds, annual expenditure nineteen six, result happiness. Annual income twenty pounds, annual expenditure twenty pounds ought and six, result misery." Whatever our expected income we must somehow adjust our scale of living to it. For nearly all couples a painful adjustment downward is necessary. We should manage and accept this in the same spirit in which we accepted some decline in sight and hearing. These declines should all be accepted as God's way for weaning us gradually from the temporal to the spiritual.

But people in the later years need very particularly to be cautioned that once they have made a sensible adjustment of living standards to probable income, they should then generously live up to it. One of the vices of old age, indeed a characteristic of senility, is an exaggerated frugality that degenerates into miserliness. Such miserliness is aggravated by the tendency that it nearly always shows its worst side toward the giving that is good and necessary for our soul. People who are too anxious about their future material security nearly always neglect their present spiritual obligations. They will feel themselves too poor to contribute to their parish or to the missions, or to provide themselves with the religious books and publications which they need to make their later years the spiritual experience they are meant to be. When after retirement our income is restricted, we need to keep before us the biblical account of the poor widow "who cast in two mites" and got our Lord's high praise for it (Mk. 12:42, 43). We can establish for ourselves the yardstick that if at any time we think we are too poor to give even the widow's mite to the Church, we have fallen into one of the ugliest symptoms of senility — miserliness.

On the reduced scale which our retired income may demand, we should nevertheless manage to engage in some social life. Retired couples should not become social recluses. If they cannot as perhaps formerly give cocktail parties or even small dinners, they certainly still can invite someone in occasionally to chat for an hour over a cup of tea or coffee. If they are friendly and make an effort to be informed and interesting they are sure to find other couples who will be glad now and then reciprocatingly to invite them for an hour over tea or coffee. It is very important for couples in the later years to maintain some social contacts. If they are new in a neighborhood, they must make an active effort to establish some social life there.

For couples who have married children with families, there is an insidious temptation to center their whole social life on them. Too concentrated a social dependence on any chosen few is always psychologically unwise. This is just as true if we lavish all our social attention on the families of our children. The exigencies of time permit only a limited amount of socializing in anyone's life. That of our married son or daughter is limited, too. Yet the young couples related to us owe it to themselves and to their children to have some social intercourse with their neighbors, their vocational associates, and their school alumni. If a young couple visits back and forth every week end with their parents, they cannot develop a well-rounded social life of their own. Eventually it may prove a strain and lead to friction and subsequent guilt feelings.

But even if young couples could and would willingly confine their social life pretty much to relatives and grandparents, it would nevertheless be unwise for elder couples to submerge their social life in their children's. They should have an independent social circle of their own. When they invite anyone it should not always exclusively be their children and other relatives. Conversely, their children should not feel that whenever they have a party they must include their parents. Obviously there are many occasions in the year, such as Christmas and birthdays, which are family days. But at other times, each generation should sometimes at least enjoy independent social get-togethers.

Even worse for elderly couples than concentrating their whole social life on their children is concentrating it on each other. This is likely to happen when a couple has no children, or none in the locality, or has moved into a strange neighborhood after retirement. Man is a social animal — and social means more than two. If a couple constitutes the sole conversation and entertainment for each other, the pair will soon seem somewhat odd to everyone else. They will become like the two inseparable cronies, one of whom said, "Everybody is becoming more and more queer, except you and me — and sometimes it seems to me you are acting a bit queer too." For normal living people need a normal set of associates. In fact, in addition to their mutual circle of friends, the husband ought to have a few cronies of his own with whom to spend an occasional afternoon or evening, and the wife ought to have a few, too.

Over and above the personal social circle, a couple ought to be active in some organization to give them a widening scope of casual acquaintances. The report on *Older People of St. Boniface Parish* (Catholic Charities, Buffalo, 1957, p. 90) finds that "the various church organizations are a ready made group" for older people to join. It holds,

> It is not wise to attempt to deal with the older aged group as a group apart. Some of the problems of aging spring from their isolation from the active, working community. Therefore attempts should be made to keep them in the larger society, rather than aiding and abetting their separateness.

Retired couples, while still in control of their own destiny, should actively participate in one or several of such wholesome organizations. There are many, as for example, the Holy Name Society, the Usher's Guild, the St. Vincent de Paul, for men; and St. Ann's Sodality, the Altar Society, the Sanctuary Society, for women.

Somewhat in short supply under Catholic auspices are societies in which couples can attend as equal partners. In the town in which I grew up men still were segregated to one side of the aisle and women to the other. Some of this tendency continues to pervade Catholic organizational life. Elderly couples especially need and want organizations which are hospitable to couples and favor the commingling of men and women.

The conventional Golden Age Clubs provide this social opportunity. Older couples, especially if they are new in a locality and lacking in social contacts, should seek out such a club or help start one. It is generally admitted that while oldsters, as was said above, should not be isolated from other age groups, there should also be some opportunities for oldsters to plan and play with fellow oldsters of both genders. Golden Age clubs and centers are seeing a remarkable growth and offer every kind of social and recreational activity. In 1957, New York had sixty such clubs. In 1959, just one section of Philadelphia, the Northeast, had fifty-four. They are variously sponsored — by community, city, lodge, or religious denomination, though so far rarely by Catholic groups. Perhaps an increased interest in our older parishioners and more active leadership and initiative on their part can help develop such Golden Age clubs under Catholic auspices.

Elderly couples, including Catholic ones, should participate in any worthy group activities calculated to enlarge the circle of acquaintances and range of interests in the later years. The reason is a very important one. It may well be that a couple feels sufficient unto each other. But unfortunately nature does not consider that a sufficient reason for allowing their idyllic existence to continue undisturbed. An elderly couple should always consciously realize that their later years are given them for the all-important purpose of preparing themselves for the next life, which either one may reach first. Therefore they should also prepare each other for the fearful eventuality of living on bravely and virtuously when God chooses to sever their happy marriage bond.

In the course of nature few couples can see the end together. In 1956, for example, there were 1,500,000 widowers, who somehow had to carry on without their spouses. And considering that the life span of women is some six years longer than men's and that most women marry men a few years older than themselves, it is not surprising that there were 4,259,000 widows. Couples in the later years should among other things make these years a preparation for each other to carry on alone when God appoints the time for one to pass away. In some cases, the loss of the partner comes as such a shock and has been so little prepared for that the survivor, so short of the goal himself, jeopardizes his salvation by committing suicide. According to insurance statistics for 1957 "the widowed had a suicide rate more than 3½ times and the divorced nearly four times that for the married." For every widowed person who goes to the extreme of suicide there are thousands and thousands dangerously depressed,

depressed beyond Christian wisdom, because they had not as couples mutually prepared themselves for the previous decease of one of them.

The later years together as a couple to be fully successful must include the mutual conditioning for the end. Each should strive to make sure that the one called to God first will have a Christian death and burial and that the one left behind will be spiritually and materially equipped to bear the loss with Christian fortitude. Each should insure that the survivor need not suffer from loneliness and friendlessness. The latter can be assured by keeping their later years as a couple enriched with a circle of good friends and acquaintances. For the former it would seem wise now and then to "meditate" aloud together on the approaching and all-important Four Last Things: death, judgment, heaven, and hell. A Christian couple ought to be able to talk about death frankly and so brace themselves mutually for it. Then the passing away of one of them is not likely to throw the other into a state of despair.

They should also betimes make a good many temporal arrangements, which can ease the last hours of the one who dies and the remaining years of the one who lives on. The most important of these is drawing a will, carefully and in detail, covering all eventualities. Every couple should periodically make wills. But certainly as they approach the last years they should make especially comprehensive ones before either is too ill to care or to understand clearly. They should also in good time arrange for a cemetery lot where someday their mortal remains may repose side by side until Gabriel blows the trumpet of the Last Judgment. All such previous arrangements lighten the worries and the burdens, if not the sorrow, of the tragic days of bereavement.

Before signs of decline or serious illness appear, both should have determined which doctor is to be called and, should it become necessary, what kind of hospitalization, if given a choice, is to be preferred. They should also establish personal contact with a priest of their parish, who can be reached directly in an emergency. The purpose of life is to merit heaven, and the later years are an especially privileged time in which a couple can fortify itself for passing from this life to the next. What, therefore is more important than staying in close touch with a Father Confessor? The greatest and last favor a husband can do for his wife or she for him is to make sure that in those last bitter moments the Father Confessor is present to administer the Last Sacraments. Then when the Lord takes the soul of the beloved one away, the sorrowing survivor has at least this shining consolation that he did his best by the other until death did them part in the one matter that counts most!

CHAPTER XI

Single or Widowed in the Later Years

FOR a married couple, while blessed with health and financial competence, the later years can easily be serene and joyous. But for widowed or divorced people, unless their relationship with their children is fortunate, and ones who have never married, unless they can share their life with a brother or sister or other close relative of their generation, the later years are a fight against loneliness, frustration, and a sense of futility.

According to *Housing the Elderly*, published by the Housing and Home Finance Agency, April, 1959, "just a fraction less than half of the men and women 65 or older are married and living with their spouse. The remainder are either widowed, separated, divorced, or unwed and constitute the group most in need of some type of housing adjustment" (p. 4). On March 19, 1958, the Bureau of the Census released a report on "Marital Status, Economic Status, and Family Status" (Series P-20, No. 81). Estimated for 1957, there were 752,000 widowers (white and nonwhite) between 65 and 74, and 878,000, 75 and over; there were 98,000 divorced, in the first, and 34,000 in the second age group; there were 80,000 separated in the first, and 24,000 in the second; and finally there were 365,000 between 65 and 74 who had never married, and 162,000 over 75 who had never married. Of the total of 4,576,000 white men between 65 and 74, 7.6 per cent had never married; of the total of 2,178,000 who were 75 and more 6.8 per cent had never married.

Correspondingly for women there were 752,000 widows (white and nonwhite) between 65 and 74, and 878,000, 75 and over;

97,000 divorced in the first and 34,000 in the second group; 38,000 separated in the first and 9000 in the second age group; and finally there were 412,000 between 65 and 74 who had never married and 246,000 over 75. Of the 5,118,000 women between 65 and 74, 7.7 per cent had never married, and 45.9 were widows; of the 2,809,000 75 and over, 8.6 per cent had never married, and 69.6 per cent were widows. All of these statistics probably include the 50,813 priests and monks and 9694 Religious Brothers; and the 164,575 Sisters (P. J. Kennedy, *Directory*, 1958). If these spiritually favored people have any special problems in the later years they are, except in a few points, not those of the laity, whom we shall mean when we speak of the unmarried.

With one exception, the problems of the single, the widowed, the divorced and separated are similar. The chief difference lies in children. People who have been parents and who in their later years have children, even if it were only to worry about them, hardly tend to feel the futility or the frustration, and seldom the loneliness of the nonmarried. Since some of their problems were suggested in the chapter on "Life as Couple" the emphasis here will be on those who must meet the later years unmarried, alone, and childless.

If in middle age, the change-of-life years are difficult for married couples, they are desperate years for the single. They may also be so for persons widowed early, who see their chances of remarriage vanishing. Most maturing bachelors and unmarried girls continue to live in a fool's paradise until their middle years. They keep looking for or waiting for the "right" one to come along to marry. They keep wishfully dreaming that having nobly waited for the "right" one so long the perfectness of their late marriage will richly compensate for the connubial bliss they missed during their thirties or forties.

One sad day as the menopause touches her in the late forties, the single woman is shaken by the realization that even if she were to find the "right" man now, their happy marriage would probably be denied the blessing of children. In the excellent pamphlet, *Why Some Women Stay Single*, Elizabeth Ogg, writes that when the realities of middle-age strike,

> An emotional tailspin is not uncommon. . . . The single woman is no exception to the cultural trend. If anything, she has greater difficulty than others in coming to terms with the aging process, because age seems to close the door finally on any hopes of marriage she may have entertained (Public Affairs Pamphlet, No. 177).

Less suddenly but none the less certainly some ten years later than for the woman, the bachelor begins to recognize such a waning in his reproductive powers (which if he was moral were a cross to him since puberty) as make him realize that even if he should now find the right girl he could give her only a limited honeymoon.

God has deigned to make the reproductive powers such a vital, almost dominant one for man and woman (as a reading of the Old Testament quickly reveals) that the positive symptoms of their waning shatters us emotionally more than the decline of any other faculty. This is true even of people who have long determined by vow or otherwise never to make use of them. The fact that we are not fully conscious of the blow to our ego or cannot bring ourselves to admit or recognize it aggravates if anything rather than alleviates the sense of missing life's major function and most thrilling experience. Biologically speaking, life's major function does wane at the change of life, and nature takes this very hard.

It requires a lot of sublimation, of substituting supernatural for natural values really to feel that life without conjugal love can be rich and rewarding. One should but cannot easily realize with Emily H. Mudd, Executive Director, Marriage Council of Philadelphia, that "Marriage should be regarded as a way of life, possibly even as a career, but surely not as a goal of life," that "many men do not marry and yet lead productive and creative lives" and "that the same can be true of women" (see Ogg, *op. cit.*, p. ii). Kathleen Rutherford, in "Vocations for the 'Purposeless Single'" (*America*, Apr., 1955) writes that Catholics think of only two vocations, married and religious, and that "The remaining alternative is reckoned unnatural, usually pretty lonely and often frustrating." She tells spinsters and bachelors, who by choice or circumstance "are denied normal marital love," that "they must make the most of the fact. Non-acceptance can only bring frustration, nerves, and unending unhappiness. Acceptance can bring the joy of a full life, a sense of high dedication. . . ."

That those involuntarily unmarried often secretly lead lives of quiet desperation would appear from the curious statistics that, excepting those in the religious state, everybody has a longer life span than single men, and that married persons have a longer life expectancy than the single, the divorced and the widowed. Census figures reported as "Marriage Increases Life Span" (UP, Dec. 11, 1941),

> the death rate for husbands between the ages of 35 and 50 is less than half that for single men. Wives 30 years and older also have a greater life expectancy than single men . . . the life expectancy of widows and widowers is approximately that of single persons. . . . The death rate of divorced persons more than 55 years old is one-third greater than that of married persons of the same age.

In "How to Stay Young" (Catholic Digest, May, 1957), John E. Gibson writes, "Studies show that bachelors and spinsters (most especially bachelors) tend to age faster and die off sooner than the rest of the population . . . the average married man has just twice the chance of attaining a hale and vigorous middle age as has the average bachelor." One can assume that irregularity of habits and inner restlessness account for the shorter life span of the unmarried. If their later years are to be reasonably content and creative, they must take pains to develop regular habits and to achieve inner acceptance of their unmarried lot.

To do the latter they must concentrate more on the ultimate purpose of life rather than on the biological one. They can keep saying to themselves that for getting to heaven, the joys of matrimony and the satisfaction of children are not necessary. They can engrave on their consciousness the words of St. Paul, "But I say to the unmarried, and to the widows: it is good for them if they so continue, even as I" (1 Cor. 7:8). As they reach the middle years, and suddenly realize that their chances of marital bliss have dropped from a probability to a very slight possibility, they can quote without quaking St. Paul's other words, "But if they do not contain themselves, let them marry. For it is better to marry than to burn." If they have waded through the turbulent passionate younger decades without having burned, if they have been chaste or celibate, even though they had not imposed upon themselves the specially meritorious vow of celibacy, God is likely to spare them in the later years most of the miseries of the sting of the flesh and keep low their cup of temptation.

It would seem that at least for Catholics who never married or are widowed when they reach the middle and later years they should give a first and serious thought to the possibility of a belated vocation. Nobody knows why millions of normal men and women, if anything even more among Catholics than among others, are denied the sacrament of matrimony. But it seems certain that many who miss it really had the gifts of character for a religious vocation. When in their forties and fifties they awaken from the dream of waiting for the "right" one to come along, they might, if encouraged, come to see that all along their vocation was not matrimony but religious celibacy. They will also find plenty of examples, some cited above in Chapter II, to tell them that, while the Church prefers early vacations, it more and more welcomes late ones. Brother Jack Greer, S.D.B., of Don Bosco College, Newton, N. J., writes,

> In more recent years, the need of priests made late vocations almost a necessity. . . . In the past few years bishops and religious superiors have recognized the wonderful results that can come from late vocations (*Catholic School Journal*, Mar., 1955).

It is true that his idea of *late* vocations is hardly as late as middle age, but the need for vocations is so great that those in the later years should be invited. Father Aloysius McDonough, C.P., writes that though there has in the past been some hesi-

tancy about accepting applicants beyond the age of 25, "Some
of the best priests and religious the Church has ever had have
been so-called late vocations" ("Late Vocations," *Sign*, Nov.,
1954). What seems to me especially suitable for people in the
later years is his suggestion that many not quite adapted for
the priestly or religious life, may "be of invaluable service to a
(religious) community . . . in the capacity of an auxiliary, an
associate."[1]

For those of us who have studied the critical and increasing
shortage of priests, Brothers, and Sisters in the mission fields,
in Latin America, in our own South and Southwest, the most
realistic hope of supplying enough workers in the vineyard is
through stimulating vocations among those in the middle and
later years. The increasing life span is making available an immense reservoir of anxious and willing human beings who need
to dedicate themselves to a noble cause, most particularly in
the later decades of their lives.

Late religious vocations seem to be in the air. They appear
to be a country-wide phenomenon among Protestants as well as
Catholics. Ecclesiastical authorities would do well to welcome
them and provide for them while the impetus lasts. An interesting article, entitled, "Parsons-Come-Lately," by Hartzell Spence
in *The Saturday Evening Post* (Aug. 29, 1959) is subtitled,
"Thousands of successful older men, finding business careers
meaningless, have started life anew as low-paid, obscure clergymen. And they've never been happier." The author says that
"The Veteran's Administration alone has given GI Bill aid for
theological education to 48,219 veterans of World War II and
Korea. Most religious seminaries have adjusted to the trend."
He instances those of the United Lutheran and the Evangelical

---

[1] For obtaining information on late vocations, Father McDonough lists:
St. Patrick's Club and Sodality for Delayed Vocations, 30 W. 16th Street
New York 11; The Seraphic Society for Vocations, St. Anthony's Monastery
151 Thompson St., New York 12; also the secular institute, *Opus Dei*, 5544
South Woodlaun Ave., Chicago 11. In Boston, the St. Philip Neri School
(126 Newbury St., Boston 16) for delayed vocations, "prepares middle-aged
men to pass seminary entrance examinations" (*Saturday Evening Post*, Aug
29, 1959).

Lutheran Churches, the American Baptist, Methodist, and the Episcopalian Churches, and adds, "The Roman Catholic Church has experienced the same phenomenon. Special organizations have been set up to encourage delayed vocations." He cites the St. Philip Neri School of Boston and the St. Patrick's Club and Sodality in New York. Of this latter he says:

> More than 300 members of this club, mostly aged forty-five to sixty, have reached ordinations as a result of the club's efforts. They include firemen, policemen, corporation presidents, and a sixty-eight-year-old public-school superintendent.

What a blessed development — this harvest of late vocations! For widows and widowers, who have outlived worthily the sacrament of matrimony, what can better crown their life than to dedicate it to the religious calling! For the single, who seem destined not to be called to the bliss of matrimony, what is more probable than that theirs was from the beginning a religious vocation? How better can they convert a life which has been purposelessly single to one of service and satisfaction as a religious in whatever capacity they may be found worthy?

Embracing the religious calling is the most final and blessed solution for all unattached people as they get on toward the later years. But precisely because it is such a high calling, a majority of the millions of single, widowed, and separated will prefer and are perhaps intended to go it alone in the secular world. Both for their happiness here and their salvation hereafter, the adjustment they make to the problems of sex is important. For women who at forty and men who at fifty have not found the "right one" to marry, it would be logical to renounce such hope for the future and creatively resolve to live single in the spirit of St. Paul's advice. However, though any chance of marriage at those ages has become highly improbable, it seems psychologically wise for most people not to suppress that slight hope ruthlessly. Its existence helps most to make life more endurable and to keep all sorts of valuable related interests alive.

In "So I'm an Old Maid," Anita Colby, at 39, advised people even though past the probability of marriage:

First, they can keep the hope of eventual marriage and a home of their own alive and burning brightly in their hearts. This is neither a foolish nor a vain hope. The daily papers frequently report instances of marriages between two older people and there's no reason why such marriages shouldn't occur more often (*Sign*, Nov., 1954).

While I would not recommend keeping the unrealistic hope of eventual marriage active and "burning brightly," I do tend to agree that for most people a continued *passive* hope makes for more healthy living. While it is somewhat ludicrous for elderly men and, perhaps worse, elderly women, to gad about actively straining belatedly to find a life's partner, and exposing themselves to many cruel rebuffs, their passive readiness to accept romance if it should happily come their way naturally would seem to be wiser for their emotional health than a bleak closing of the door of hope.

Miss Colby is right in holding that there is no reason why marriages among the elderly should not occur more often. They would at least moderately increase if they got a fraction of the encouragement in art and literature given to romance among the young. Professor Drake comments as follows on old persons marrying, "Our society generally frowns on these marriages or ridicules those who marry well after the prime of life has been passed. For some reason sex activity or the thought of it in older people seems repulsive or 'indecent' to many young persons" (*op. cit.*, p. 316). Nature unfortunately abets this prejudice. Whereas it endows the young with so much sex appeal that everybody feels attracted to them and they to each other, it progressively takes this mysterious appeal away from people as they grow older until in the later years they have little for anybody. Almost as if only by a special concession it allows it to survive mutually in married couples in whom the romantic impulse of their youth blessedly carries into the later years.

From a worldly viewpoint, it is the tragedy of the later years that there are millions of marriageable men and women in their sixties and seventies secretly anxious to marry but except in a few newsworthy instances incapable of being romantically attracted to one another. From a spiritual viewpoint, of course, this mutual lack of sex appeal in old age greatly eases the thorny path to salvation. After a life time of praying, "Lead us not into temptation," the Lord goes a long way to grant our prayer!

When Dr. Heidegger, in Hawthorne's story, called in the three septuagenarians and the widow for his rejuvenating experiment, all four were at ease, without a trace of passion or jealousy. But as soon as his liquid had made them young again, the men recovered their libido and the woman her "charm," and in a matter of moments rivalry and jealousy and fighting sullied the room. While the erstwhile sex appeal was revived, the four could not be calm and wise! Dr. Heidegger refused them more of the liquid and was glad to have them old again — free from desire and jealousy.

It is evidently in God's plan that in the later years, whatever other charms people retain, the quality best described as sex appeal is so drained away that it seldom touches spark enough in two elderly people to marry. But the fact that He permitted it to happen at all should induce us to encourage it whenever there is a likelihood. If only because in the later years two certainly can live cheaper than one, late marriage might well be encouraged. But also such marriages are an emotional and moral boon to the lucky participants. It would be well if society could produce a more congenial setting for promoting them. They should be encouraged even if they must usually be founded more on affection and convenience than on romantic love.

At any rate, whoever wants to help people in the later years socially must do so on the basis of the commingling of the sexes. One must recognize that the sexes are a very important social complement to one another. It is not good for men to be alone, nor for women. The farther the likelihood of marriage recedes the more are opportunities needed where men and women can talk and work and play together. Stag parties and hen parties are good for the young; in the old they encourage senility. In *When Parents Grow Old*, Elizabeth Ogg, pleading for a normal social life for oldsters, writes:

An intelligent, 70-year-old widow said of a golden-age club: "I don't think you can appreciate what it means to be able to sit down to a table and have a conversation with a man. All I see most of the time are women. At my age, I can't go places in the evening where men are, so I stay home." (Public Affair Pamphlet No. 208).

Society should even encourage twosome friendships among the elderly and expect them to be and remain merely platonic. When two young people date each other, society is right in expecting a proximate marriage announcement or in suspecting sin. But people in the later years must not be supposed to be motivated by romantic desires when they seek each other's company. They need mixed company, however platonic it remains, for reasonably full and happy living. If two such friends were tempted enough for sin, they could be assumed to be more than willing also to marry.

In short, unmarried people in their later years should make sure their social circle includes some persons of the opposite sex. Their families, the Church, the community should provide opportunities where oldsters of both sexes can meet together. While the primary purpose should be merely platonic companionship, the secondary one of a possible romantic attachment now and again should be welcomed but not expected.

Naturally unmarried elders, like married couples, should try to be economically useful as long as possible. They should keep at their trade or profession as long as circumstances permit. As a matter of fact, it is recommended especially for the unattached and never-married to dedicate themselves to their work, to make it a means not only of earning a living but of helping get the world's work done. Once retired, they should even more than other oldsters try to get some part-time work if at all possible, or develop some avocation or hobby.

But next to the acceptance of sexual unfulfillment, the most important problem for the unmarried elder is that of living arrangements. Professor Drake writes, "Most old people who are married live with their spouses. Nonmarried elders live alone, with relatives, or as unrelated individuals in boarding houses, hotels, or institutions" (*op. cit.*, p. 55). Another study, *Housing for the Elderly* (p. 5), reports that close to 70 per cent of couples maintain their home, about 25 per cent live with children, and about 5 per cent have some special or institutionalized living arrangements. However,

> Among the unrelated individuals — the widows and widowers, spinsters and bachelors — the proportion who maintain their own homes drops sharply to 50 per cent among the men and 40 per cent among the women. Conversely, the proportion living with children rises to 31 per cent among the men, 45 per cent among the women.

Of these types of living arrangement the most desirable, emotionally, morally, and economically for the single, is in the home of interested relatives. According to the Bureau of Census "about three million older people are living in the homes of married children or other close relatives." While living with relatives presents a challenge, it is also "an opportunity to make a substantial contribution to a better life in the later years" (*The Older Person in the Home*, Public Health Service, 1957). Generally speaking, Social Security, while it may not be adequate to maintain a separate apartment, does enable an oldster to have relatives house him at perhaps even a modest profit to themselves. Emotionally, in the bosom of such a household, he has considerable insurance against loneliness, and they have the benefit of his wisdom — and perhaps his baby sitting!

Morally, few things keep any of us straight so well as the eyes of watchful and kindly relatives. An oldster alone in a boarding house or apartment can take to tippling much more readily than in the house of his daughter or his niece! More specifically, we have data that oldsters in the homes of relatives go to church more than those who live alone. It is sad to think that as people come nearer to their eternal home they tend to visit God's earthly tabernacle rather less than more. *Organized Religion and the Older Person* (University of Florida Press, 1958, p. 59) reports:

Older lone persons go less [to Church] than any other group in that only 21 per cent attend regularly . . . other studies confirm the findings that in later years couples and widowed and lone people cut down on the frequency of church attendance.

Interestingly, this study calls for further research "to learn to what extent the presence of older children and other adults stimulates older people to attend regularly." What Catholic studies we have also suggest that elder Catholics are more likely to attend Sunday Mass if some interested relative urges them and perhaps takes them. Studies also indicate that older women remain "more active in religion than do older men" (*ibid.,* p. 27). And one also notes that whereas only 31 per cent of lone men live with their children, 45 per cent of lone elderly women do. Perhaps we are further justified in suggesting parenthetically that possibly women tend to outlive men by some six years because in their later years they more often live with their children — and go to Church more!

In short, emotionally and morally, lucky are the lone oldsters who can find a room with close relatives. The whole world feels more at ease knowing that Chancellor Adenauer, octogenarian widower, is sharing his villa with his married daughter than if he were alone in some apartment or hotel! But an older person in the home must have a certain minimum of comforts and privacy. He must have a room by himself, large enough to serve as bedroom and living room. It should have a radio or television, and be suitable for inviting a few cronies on occasion for a game of cards or for conversation. The room must be easily heated in the winter, and easily ventilated in the summer. It is well if the furniture includes some of an oldster's own pieces especially treasured from former days, even if they do not perfectly match the rest. A bathroom must be near on the same floor. In general, the fewer the stairs the better. In some cases a first floor room may be essential.

Before such living arrangements are undertaken, it were well for the good of both parties to agree on some ground rules, for example, as to keeping the room clean, a regular schedule for meals, an understanding about presence at company, and so on. What is made clear beforehand and agreed upon, seldom creates serious friction afterward. If such an arrangement is undertaken in the right spirit, an older relative in the house can be a blessing all around. But like every other human arrangement, it will entail some problems and difficulties. It is in overcoming these intelligently that we develop our characters and merit grace in the eyes of God.

According to figures adduced, some 50 per cent of unmarried men and 40 per cent of women keep their own homes or apartments. Widows and widowers, especially if they still have unmarried children, should keep up their own households. Widows, even when their children are gone, can sometimes wisely keep their household if they rent out rooms or share the dwelling and the expenses with another woman. For unmarried men and women, an independent house or apartment is expensive, emotionally conducive to loneliness, and morally problematic. But professional people, of more than average income, who have long had their own house or apartment, and perhaps for prestige reasons need it, will hardly be willing to give it up while still well enough to manage it. Their inclination must be respected.

Sociologists at present encourage people to fend for themselves in their own homes or apartments as long as possible. Even when they get too weak or ill to manage completely by themselves, social agencies are developing various types of homemaker services for them. A trained homemaker comes for several hours a day or a few times a week and provides such personal services, as bedside care, food, laundry, and light cleaning. This is a type of service for older people that deserves to be encouraged.

After a lone person is no longer willing or able to maintain his own house or apartment, increasingly more alternatives are developing. The fact that Social Security is giving virtually everyone in the later years the certain means to pay at least a modest sum for keep is making it feasible to establish various types of old-age homes and hotels. Actually only a small percentage of people in their later years need and want such institutions. But their very existence gives the soothing assurance that if one should ever need nursing and medical care and could not manage by oneself, there are enough good places that will accept the old and sick.

Catholics have always recognized the need for old-age homes for at least a minority of the aged. In 1910 Catholics maintained 98 such homes in this country, 142 in 1930, and 171 in 1940. In recent years the rate of establishment of such homes has accelerated. By 1958 there were 314 Catholic homes of the aged with 27,890 guests.[2] With the tremendous increase in the number of people over 65, with their guarantee of some minimum income from Social Security, one can hope for an imaginative expansion in various types of homes and hotels for people in the later years, not only under state and secular, but especially also under Catholic auspices. Since getting ready for heaven must be the chief purpose of the later years, where better can this goal be secured for Catholic oldsters than in Catholic homes for the aged?

For those who must negotiate the later years alone, without spouse or children, it becomes all the more necessary, while still clearheaded and energetic, to make arrangements for a holy and Christian death and burial. Like everyone else, we should also betimes make a careful will. And since there will probably be few relatives to pray for our souls after our passing, we should even more than others think of remembering in our will religious institutions, which keep sending prayers up to God for their benefactors. Perhaps since we could not give children to Church and country, we can modestly compensate for this want by the use we make of the worldly goods God let us acquire. We cannot take them with us, but we can keep them doing much good if we will them to the Church and her missions.

Finally, however much it may pain us to think of our terminal or last illness, we should, since it is inevitable, make sure that when it comes, there will be not only a good doctor to take care

---

[2] See the author's, "The Catholic Stake in the Aged," *Social Justice Review*, Jan., 1959.

of us but a kindly priest to give us the Last Sacraments and to bury us with all the Catholic rites.

This whole matter of the later years, even if we are unmarried or widowed, simply will not be such a lonely or unhappy time if we keep thinking of them as the high road on the last lap to our eternal salvation. To get to heaven we don't need a spouse, we don't need children or heirs, we don't need good health — all we need is the state of sanctifying grace!

CHAPTER XII

Being a Venerable Relative

A WISE elder relative is one of the greatest blessings a family can have. "Grandparents," someone wrote, "are needed to add a greater measure of that priceless ingredient of emotional health. . . . Grandparents also help a child's emotional development by widening the circle in which children feel at home. . . . The older generation makes a contribution in widening the horizon of a child's mind as well as his feelings."[1] An elder relative widens the whole family circle, deepens it by a whole generation, and brings to it the perspective of half a century or more. An elder relative may be so by virtue of several possible relationships, from grandparents to parents-in-law. Each relationship has its own aspects, values and advantages, and also special requirements and problems.

But some generalizations can be set down for all of them.

Elder relatives must keep and look as fit as nature permits. They should not make their age an excuse for not doing for themselves what they still can. Even when ill, they should within the limits of a doctor's orders be as self-reliant as possible. People respect pluck — in the old no less than in the young. It is also the best therapy. The best way to stay healthy is to act healthy; and the best way when sick to get well again is to do for oneself just as much as the doctor allows.

Elder relatives must keep up their appearance. They may really no longer care how they look — they no longer hope for fame or

---

[1] Edith G. Neisser, *How to be a good Mother-in-Law and Grandmother*, Public Affairs Pamphlet No. 174, July, 1956, pp. 15–18.

romance. But their children, grandchildren, nieces and nephews do still hope for them. An elder relative who looks dowdy or behind the times reflects on them. They will find it hard to love and respect someone of whom before neighbors they must feel ashamed. Dr. William B. Terhune in *Harvest Years* tells oldsters:

> Take renewed interest in the improvement of posture and gait: you will look and feel better. Be immaculately groomed. . . . Take good care of your hair. . . . A man must shave *carefully* daily. When you dress, wear your glasses — no frayed shirts, no spots. Keep your clothes meticulously clean and pressed (The Silver Hill Foundation, New Canaan, Conn., 1954).

Elder relatives should watch their fashions so that no one can say of them what Holmes said of the old veteran who provoked a grin because "the old three-cornered hat, / And the breeches, — and all that" were so queer!

Even more than their dress and manners should their language and ideas stay plastic and up-to-date. Rigidity of mental outlook must continually be fought back. For their mental health and intellectual respectability, elder relatives must keep up with events. They should read a daily paper, a weekly diocesan paper, and at least one good news magazine such as *U. S. News*, *Newsweek*, or *Time*. Who reads timely material will not stagnate mentally, or live narrowly in the past, but will be able to give the younger generation a good run of conversational change. Few in the later years nowadays need to be urged to watch television or listen to the radio, which most incline to do too much. But they might be urged to keep trying to elevate their taste in programs, to patronize more challenging ones — those consisting of better news, finer music, greater drama. Persons of any age who have inside information or the latest or a lot of it are welcome and popular. Next to the parish church, the place elder relatives should know best is the neighborhood library.

One's role as an elder relative naturally depends a lot on circumstances and proximity. If we are separated by too great a distance for frequent visiting, we should enthusiastically play our role by correspondence. One could wax eloquent on the almost infallible means a friendly letter provides for giving joy to the recipient. We can be certain if we send our younger relatives even tolerably interesting and legible letters we will never wear the welcome of them thin. Letters written with the intent of interesting the recipients, which means to please the reader more than relieve the writer, are always treasured. Really venerable relatives write newsy letters without expecting an answer every time or feeling hurt if there is no quick acknowledgment. We should learn to word our letters so that each one does not call for an answer, for sending a letter requiring an answer is somewhat of an imposition. In our later years we very likely have much more time to write than those in the thick of life's battles. Let us honestly try to cheer them up with our missives and be satisfied with cheery acknowledgments now and then. These, though few, will be worth their weight in gold, for few things give more cheer and so dispel loneliness than a postman walking up waving a letter at us.

If we live in the same locality near enough for frequent visits, our role of venerable relative is of course richer but also more delicate. It takes a certain amount of fine instinct to keep mutual visits the right frequency and duration. While elder relatives might conveniently extend a blanket invitation to drop in any time, they should not themselves expect such an invitation or presume such a one on the part of the younger generation. Most of all, as was indicated in previous chapters, they should not expect to be invited to every party their young relatives give. In fact, they themselves should cultivate enough of a circle of friends now and then to have a party in which their younger relatives are not expected. Among relatives as among others, the secret of being welcome lies in not being available all the time nor expecting to be welcome at any and all moments. People in the later years need to guard against becoming emotionally so wrapped up in their younger relatives as to have time for nobody else and to give them no time for friends of their own. When the proper frequency of visits cannot be felt intuitively, it is best simply to determine it by talking the matter over from time to time.

The richest role of a venerable relative is possible when living under the same roof. Also, as everywhere in life, the closer the contact the more tact, wisdom, and forbearance are required for achieving a maximum of good feelings. It is essential that a room arrangement is possible permitting of some mutual privacy. It is also important that duties and privileges be clearly defined and understood. If for example a grandmother is to help in the kitchen, then a clear division of tasks between her and the house-wife should be drawn. A time schedule for certain functions and use of facilities should be agreed upon. Generally what is quietly discussed ahead of time and agreed upon is likely to cause no friction later. If points of friction arise at any time, they should immediately be presented for discussion rather than allowed to build up suppressed blood pressure.

It seems that the most difficult venerable relative relationship is that of mother-in-law — whether in the same house, or within visiting or only within letter-writing distance. This may be partly due to the fact that mothers-in-law have had a bad press, that it has for decades been somewhat fashionable to glorify mothers but to depreciate them as mothers-in-law. They have thus perhaps become something like lightning rods for the natural frictions and tensions of young couples. Instead of putting the blame where it belongs, on themselves, they make the mothers-in-law the scapegoats. The latter may thus be serving a valuable if thankless function.

It suggests as a first policy that mothers-in-law should not take to heart every disparaging remark directed to them by their in-laws. They should realize that they are merely the victims of blowing off steam, not meant to hurt them. That takes nobility of nature but not more than is implied in the words of St. Francis, "Lord, grant that I may seek rather to comfort than be comforted . . . To love than be loved."

Their second and almost invincible policy should be that they determine in their hearts to love rather than demand to be loved. By instinct both animals and human beings sense whether someone really likes them deep down in their heart or merely acts friendly. When we sincerely from the bottom of our hearts like anyone nature virtually compels that person soon to like us too. It is thought that very many mothers at the beginning secretly resent the one who takes their daughter or son away from them in marriage. That it is not naturally easy for parents to give up their children in marriage appears from the repeated biblical injunction that a man shall "leave father and mother, and shall cleave to his wife" (Mt. 19:5).

While parents will not consciously admit such resentment even to themselves, it shows through in expressions like, "Of course, our son should marry, but not yet," or, "He needs a more mature girl for a wife. . . ." A daughter-in-law or son-in-law instinctively, despite polite words and acts, senses being not really welcome, develops fear of her in-laws, and fear breeds dislike. As a preliminary to being liked, therefore, a mother-in-law must use on herself all the charity and psychology possible to bring herself around to really, honestly liking the one who married her child and truly wishing that one well, well as they see and want it. Without this inner conversion, a mother-in-law cannot really win the love and confidence of her child's spouse; with it, she is almost certain to do so.

For any elder relatives, just as for a mother-in-law the basic requirement of being liked and being listened to is to have deep good will and affection for the younger generations, including the in-laws. Good will begets good will.

But our sincere interest in their welfare must not lead us to anxious meddling in their lives. We must not consider it our responsibility to keep them from making any mistakes, perhaps the same mistakes we once made. We must accept the law of life that each generation must work out its own salvation. We must stand by silently, if in agony, as those we love bruise themselves in trial and error while they grope for skill and wisdom. In small things and big, we must more or less let them be on their own. Surely grandmother can bake a cake better than granddaughter, grandfather can pull in the fish better than grandson; but the young ones, except for some tactful hints, must be allowed to try these things themselves. Just as even at the risk of bumps and accidents, one can only learn to drive by driving, so one can learn to live only by living under one's own power, mistakes and all. To make fatal accidents unlikely (not impossible) while learning to drive, and to make mortal sins improbable (not impossible) while growing up, young people are given some preliminary lessons and instructions. But essentially, courtship, marriage, livelihood, like learning to drive, must be mastered by each generation itself. It cannot be done for them.

That is very hard for anxious, well-meaning elder relatives to recognize and to practice. But it must be done, if we want to be a wholesome and welcome influence. God could prevent sin with one stroke — by simply taking away our free will. But though He loves us dearly, He suffers us to be on our own. If we get irrevocably lost, He constrains Himself to permit the tragedy. But if we come through bruised perhaps but safely, He will rejoice at the reward we have deserved by our own efforts. Somewhat similarly we must feel about our younger relatives. One may keep praying that they do the right thing but one may not nag them into it. Let the young daughter-in-law burn the toast at the beginning; toasting it for her will hardly help her become a good cook. Let the son-in-law lay out his shop in the cellar wrong — it will not be his last house to do better with. Of course, one advises them, one tries gently to keep them from pitfalls; and one is absolutely firm when it is a matter of life and death. But in general we should not consider our responsibility to correct our relatives much more peremptory than that to correct anyone else. We should not become personal or emotional about it. If we do, we will seem to be more intent upon pleasing ourselves than on genuinely helping them.

A few general precepts regarding especially younger in-laws. It is usually wise not to participate in their arguments. Young couples will argue and thereby smooth the edges off their per-

sonalities. By taking sides we merely add a sour foreign note.
It stands to reason that we should make it a point never to
stir up trouble between couples. As an example of what one
should not do, Edith G. Neisser cites a mother's reproaching
the son-in-law by saying to her daughter, "If I were you, I
wouldn't stand for it. You don't have to be a doormat" (*How
to be a good Mother-in-law*, p. 9). We should make it a rule
never to say to one what we would not be willing to say to
both. Older relatives must accept the fact, however hard it may
be, that when a daughter, son, niece, or nephew marries, he or
she owes the first loyalty to the spouse, not to us, and that includes the sharing of confidences. The best way to get along with
younger relatives is to do more to help them get along among
themselves than specifically to like us.

Perhaps the most pervasive pitfall for a somewhat lonely elder
relative is to feel sorry for himself. If we feel sorry for ourselves
we cannot be lovable and gracious. Elder relatives should guard
themselves against this at all times. Such remarks as, "Nobody
bothers when you're old," or, "Guess you don't want granny
around when you're having a good time," or, "Please, don't let
me spoil your fun," even when said smilingly, carry the implication of feeling sorry for ourselves. This feeling comes from a
basic selfishness; it is a sign that some of the Old Adam is
still in us. Our Lord was not sorry for himself — not even on
his Way of the Cross. If we have the right spiritual outlook, if
we look on the later years as planks to heaven, we will graciously,
uncomplainingly accept the little neglects we suffer or fancy
we suffer. We will be so concerned about seeing others happy
that we will hardly take note of what might be slights. It can
be assumed that most slights are unintentional. Even if on
occasion they are real, perhaps they are deserved, and can help
us to perfect ourselves.

Elder relatives who are well adjusted, who are spiritually
oriented, are sincerely Assisian, seeking "rather to comfort than
be comforted; / To understand rather than be understood." They
will with all their heart and mind try to sense what is the real

wish and pleasure of others and what is to their advantage. If our younger relatives really want us along, we will go; if not, we will not. We will then decline graciously but firmly, saying perhaps, "No, thank you, but I will watch television." This sort of answer avoids the possible dishonesty or rudeness of saying, "No, I do not want to go." By no means should we answer in a sorry-for-ourselves manner, such as, "Oh, you will be happier without me, I am sure." We should never decline an invitation in a manner which is likely to put before people the alternative of being either dishonest or rude. To do so is a prize bit of the selfishness of the Old Adam. It is also a sure way to make others uncomfortable and unhappy on account of us.

Elder relatives should adjust the topics and the timing of their speech to the wishes and needs of others. It is somewhat proverbial that in the later years people tend to ramble on about the exploits of their youth. Instead of talking about their own youth it would be better for them to talk about the youth of their younger relatives. They will be appreciated if they recall to grandchildren instances in their childhood and in that of their parents. If elder relatives can submerge the "ego" in their stories of the past, they can give the young generation a valuable sense of history. They should not however keep extolling the good old days to the disparagement of the present. Judicious comparisons, based on reality, not on false memories, may well be made, but to help the young we must not dwell in the past. Their life is now. Whatever we relate must have a bearing on the present and the future. Nor should we dwell too much on sorrows and misfortunes, least of all upon our own aches and pains. We should detail them to our doctor, but at home allude to them only rarely and then under the guidance of good taste.

While an elder relative will be very slow to criticize anything, he will always do so in a tactful, loving manner, never in an irritable, disgusted tone. As Norah Smaridge wrote in a humorous article entitled, "How to Be a Good Aunt" (*Ave Maria*, June 28, 1958), "Nagging is expected from mothers but is not to be tolerated in aunts. A good aunt does not fuss about things . . .

is not horrified by a big appetite . . . never gives your mother advice about you. . . . The one thing she never does is spy on you, and tell your mother." Nevertheless, in matters of right and wrong, elder relatives should stand as norms. They should promote proper conduct wisely, and prevent improper conduct tactfully but firmly and clearly show their disapproval of sinful conduct.

In most well-regulated or religious families, friction is likely to develop not so much in clear matters of right and wrong but in matters of customs and manners. Social customs change all the time: even the most modest bathing suit of today would have been considered grossly indecent fifty years ago. In scores of matters like this, elder relatives must recognize that the prime responsibility lies with the parents of children, not with us. We may tactfully at the proper time voice our attitude on such a matter, but we should never be dogmatic, inflexible, self-right-eously condemnatory. We should distinguish clearly between what is a sin and what is only a temptation. The latter vary in degree with individuals and cultures. An unchaperoned date was once considered an irresistible temptation to mortal sin. Now in this country even the best Catholic circles approve of such dating. Therefore in any matters of this type we should be very circumspect.

With anyone, with our equals, with in-law, and even with young children, we do well if we talk facts rather than opinions, if we reason rather than dogmatize. We should present the facts and reasons which are the basis of our advice. We should not even expect children to feel anything but frustrated if the only reason we give them is the word *because*. We should not use our prerogative of elder relative to talk down to the young generation, not even to the children. It would seem to be wisest to adopt a tone of man to man or woman to woman with them. When Holmes in his eighties, was sitting on the porch discussing life with Betsy Warder, aged 16, he said "I won't refrain from talking about anything because you're too young, if you won't because I'm too old."

Elder relatives will normally be great hits with young children and can be of inestimable value to them. The old and the very young somehow get along well together. It comes so naturally to them that grandparents need little advice on how to manage their young grandchildren. When the latter get into their teens, they often are more difficult to handle and challenge all the understanding and wisdom elders can muster.

Children, both before and during their teens, have so very much to learn, so many good habits to acquire and bad ones to shun, that elder relatives who are near them can be one of life's greatest blessings. Parents usually have their hands full making a living, providing the necessities. An elder relative, no longer so involved, and wise with the years and experienced, can impart all sorts of skills and tricks and knowledge. I grew up on a farm, but because I had no elder relative to spend the young lazy days with me, and because my parents were far too busy for such trifles, I saw hundreds of wild flowers and shrubs and trees, but unfortunately never learned their names. How much it would have enriched my life had a grandfather taught me the names of this vegetation. My brother and I learned swimming and skating and angling the clumsy way. A grandfather could have tipped us off to the right way. In prep school I felt stupid never at home to have learned checkers or chess or even the simpler card games. Surely any elder relative would have supplied that awkward deficiency.

For hundreds of things involving sports, machines, natural science, which a boy can absorb from a grandfather or grand-uncle, there must be at least as many which a girl can learn from a grandmother or grandaunt. An elder relative should con-sider imparting such skills and knowledge as a valuable mission; should consciously and deliberately improve every occasion to do so. That may also give him a valuable motive for keeping his own skills and knowledge alive. He may find it necessary to brush up on this or that at an adult evening school or Golden Age Club. If so he is taking out an excellent insurance against senility, against the decline of his own mind. As grandchildren get into the higher grades they will certainly appreciate a chance to discuss their schoolwork with an elder relative who is knowledgeable. Such a relative will of course not undermine the morale of the school, he will not exalt the methods of the past to the disparagement of those of today. He will realize that many things have changed, including rules of grammar and of punctuation. He will therefore proffer his knowledge tactfully, with a view not to show how smart he himself is but to be of real help to his young charge.

If an elder relative is not entirely destitute, he can give his juvenile relatives very much pleasure with very little means. He can thrill them with a dime more at four than with a dollar at sixteen. In the playful article, "How to Be a Good Aunt," by Norah Smaridge, a good aunt "buys tickets off you . . . saves coupons for you . . . gives you things you *want* on your birthday, which are not handkerchiefs or underwear." She knows a boy cannot "have too many ray guns and space helmets" and already has "enough *books*." Nevertheless I would make a plea for giving our young relatives *books* — any gifts with a learning factor, which children may not fully appreciate at the time but be grateful for later.

With a book, for example, there is always a chance that a spark may be struck that lasts for life. Literally, the gift as a boy I remember most gratefully, was an illustrated copy of Rip van Winkle an uncle in Milwaukee brought one day. Barely able to read, I would certainly not have had sense enough to ask for this as a gift. Yet once I had it, I read it; it made an in- delible impression on me, and made me hospitable to books ever after. Elder relatives have a heavenly chance, with even small means, to provide for their juvenile relatives not only much joy but rich new horizons — if they choose gifts with an eye to helping them grow both in body and mind.

Indeed, elder relatives can be any family's greatest blessing. Their mature wisdom, distilled in tactful advice, can make the whole family happier and better. If they do not obtrude themselves, yet are not embarrassingly self-effacing, if they honestly want to be of service but do not expect vocal appreciation all the time, they will be loved and valued by any family. They will be a comfort to everybody, and when their strength someday fails, they will have a whole family ready and anxious to comfort them.

CHAPTER XIII

Being an "Elder" Citizen

A VENERABLE relative is also a senior citizen and should be an "elder" one, meaning a wise and helpful one. Clark Tibbitts, assistant director, Special Staff on Aging of the U. S. Department of Health, Education, and Welfare, in an essay entitled, "Aging as a Modern Social Achievement," writes,

> Indeed, aging may best be defined as the survival of a growing number of people who have completed the traditional adult roles of making a living and child-rearing.[1]

He calls the presence now of nearly fifty million persons over forty-five "who are reasonably certain of a good many years of free time in the future" as "an unprecedented achievement . . . the adult years have been lengthened and may now be divided into more or less distinct phases; or, perhaps better, an entirely new period has been added to life." In this new period, which we can label from 65 to 85, he says:

> Many people are finding their way to rich adventure. . . . Some intensify their contributions to community activities, some turn to educational activities to clarify and amplify their understanding of the life of mankind and themselves, some seek to sharpen their perceptions in the arts by cultivating an interest in literature, painting, and music. Some seek to express themselves in the arts and crafts. Some turn to a mixture of these things and further spice it up by travel (p. 28).

Dr. John E. Anderson, former director of Child Welfare at the University of Minnesota, in "Psychological Aspects of Free Time," writes that the man at sixty-five faces "the same problem

---

[1] In *Free Time: Challenge to Later Maturity*, edited by Donahue, Hunter, Coons, and Maurice, The University of Michigan Press, Ann Arbor, 1958, p. 18.

that the married woman faces fifteen or twenty years earlier when she finds her children gone and her household restricted to her husband and herself." She then has to find substitute activities outside the home:

> Many women develop interests in community, philanthropic, religious, or social activities. In fact, a large proportion of the voluntary programs in our modern society are carried on by women who have made this transition (see *Free Time*, p. 35).

Any of us who have tried to promote cultural or civic activities have gratefully noticed that but for the help of these mature women such activities in modern America would not succeed.

Perhaps men in the high tide of their careers just do not have the time and energy for culture or public affairs. But what a glorious opportunity of useful service can be theirs when they do reach the later years, freed from pressing economic responsibilities!

Youth is idealistic, but also rash, inconsiderate, radical. Senior citizens have learned from history and experience that the most idealistic reforms, if violent, do more harm than good. They have learned that one must keep trying to make the world better but must do it patiently. By their sheer numbers — fifty million over 45, fifteen million over 64 — they are a tremendous power, the more so since the right to vote, which is not given until 21, continues intact to the end of life. The Welfare Commissioner of New York City, recalling that in that city with a voting population of two and a half million, a million are over sixty, said, "If the aged ever united on their needs, they would be the most potent force in the city, state, or nation" (*New York Times*, Mar. 3, 1958). This tremendous voting power, seconded by considerable financial assets, should be expected to be somewhat of a balance wheel in our democracy. It should throw its immense weight against dangerous, possibly tragic experiments to the left or to the right.

But what should be is not always what is. The senior citizens under the spell of a demagogue could well become a destructive selfish force, one out to advance only its own interest to the harm and ultimate revolt of the productive population in the younger ages. One recalls the development into a powerful political pressure group of the Townsend Plan of the thirties. In 1933, Everett Townsend, the retired physician, proposed monthly pensions of $200 a month to citizens over 60, the money to be spent within the month and to be derived from a two per cent transaction tax. Though competent economists united in calling the plan unsound, it nevertheless came repeatedly before Congress. Someday a selfish and perhaps ruinous proposal, by including in the bribe enough of the voters not yet 65, might be steamrollered into a law. It is incumbent therefore on all senior citizens to become interested in public affairs, to inform themselves as to what is best, not only for themselves but for God and country.

Senior citizens ought to belong to and work through organizations. This is for their own good and for that of society. Professor Ernest W. Burgess, Emeritus, University of Chicago, in "The Retired Person and Organizational Activities," points out:

> Man has always been a group being. But modern man is becoming more and more an organization man. . . . Men and women have to depend more and more on organizations and often on large organizations to find work, to gain security, to play, and to worship. The family has contracted in relative importance. Outside of an organization a person tends to be useless and impotent (see *Free Time*, pp. 151–152).

He finds that in a study of nearly 3000 older persons, those who were active in organizations "showed the superior social adjustment," and holds that only through participation in organizations can most older persons realize "the potential values of retirement living."

While our senior citizens should belong to general organizations, they should especially be interested in those serving the later years. Professor Burgess holds that while they should participate "in organizations serving different ages . . . most retired persons find satisfaction in belonging to groups made up of their peers." We have proof of this, he thinks, in "the rapid growth in recent years of day centers, golden-age clubs, senior citizens' groups, and others by different names" (see *Free Time*, p. 155).

It should probably be emphasized that in such organizations "the older people should participate in planning the activities." The fifteen million people 65 and over represent an enormous potential of experience and know-how. Certainly they should be able to develop and to manage and for the most part to service desirable organizations of senior citizens. Every community might well have a golden-age club or its equivalent. Such clubs might be organized along geographic, professional, or denominational lines, including both men and women. Catholic senior citizens should easily be able to get together and with the blessings of the pastor organize such clubs, utilizing the parish facilities on afternoons or evenings when these are available. With meetings at least once a month, preferably once a week, these older citizens could dispel a feeling of loneliness and find precisely the companionship suitable for the twilight years between earth and heaven. As an important value, they should administer the club themselves — to keep alive the sense and the capacity of social responsibility. The modest refreshments, like coffee and doughnuts, all can co-operate in supplying and in serving.

Senior citizens can also move to establish day or recreational centers for themselves. Dr. Shock writes that in addition to sixty Golden Age Clubs in New York City "there were 17 day centers for the elderly, which had some 6000 enrolled members" (*Trends*, p. 107). Whereas clubs have limited programs and only one or two meetings a week, centers tend to have all-day activities four or more days a week. Such centers need some trained personnel, perhaps a full-time, paid supervisor. Among fifteen million senior citizens, many ought to have the professional training to supply this personnel. Such day centers offer social activities of all kinds, social contacts, and opportunities for group participation. They offer "such diverse activities as writing, painting, woodworking, embroidery, choral singing, and dramatics."

Among the important values of such clubs and centers should be that they will give oldsters not only recreational and social activities, but the opportunity to organize, discuss, and serve —

according to abilities, tastes, and circumstances. Miss Georgene
E. Bowen, consultant on recreation, Division of Health and Welfare, Philadelphia, encourages member participation of any kind,
on any level. They can help, for example, in sending out notices,
preparing and serving refreshments, setting up chairs and tables,
washing dishes and cleaning up, arranging flowers, writing letters
and birthday cards to absent members; a few can serve as
librarians, secretaries, treasurers; those who are musicians, artists,
writers, etc., should have their talents used.[2]

An enthusiastic pioneer in organizing old-age activities among
Catholics is Father W. F. Suedkamp, Secretary of Catholic Charities, Detroit, Michigan. As leader of the workshop on "Programs
for the Aged," 1959 National Convention of the National Council of Catholic Men (Apr. 4, 1959), he outlined the efforts in
Detroit. Acquiring on old building downtown, he opened a Day
Care Center, where elderly people could drop in for a cup of tea
and conversation. He had wondered whether oldsters would come,
but "They came in droves — brought problems with them too."
Since housing was one of the chief problems, the 750 room
hotel "Detroiter" was bought and remodeled. In it a day center
for oldsters in the neighborhood was established. The next easy
step was a senior arts and crafts program. Though, according to
Father Suedkamp, only one in ten can make anything usable
or beautiful, for those who can, such a program is a godsend. It
led to the opening of a shop, managed by one of the senior citizens, where the products could be sold. Father Suedkamp found
that once real interest in the older persons is aroused in a parish,
it gains momentum. For example, he had congratulations sent
to all couples mentioned in the paper as celebrating their golden
wedding, organized a golden wedding ball, and sent them free
tickets. Eight hundred attended.

---

[2] See "Salient Points on Organization of Clubs for Older People," by
Georgene E. Bowen, Health and Welfare Council, 1617 Pennsylvania Blvd.,
Philadelphia 3, Pa., five-page mimeographed pamphlet, full of excellent helps
for starting old-age clubs or centers. Also helpful is "A Treasury of Program
Ideas for Clubs of Older People," Feb., 1956, 6 pp., obtainable from the
Health and Welfare Council, 311 South Juniper St., Philadelphia 7, Pa.

Programs like this senior citizens should be able to initiate and largely carry out themselves. For much of the work they should contribute their services voluntarily; posts and duties requiring pay should whenever feasible be given to the qualified senior citizens among them.

In some communities summer vacations for older persons are arranged. Often it is relatively inexpensive to rent the facilities of children's camps by the day or the week at the end of the regular seasons. One of the most humanitarian programs elder citizens can initiate is friendly visiting of their less ambulant fellow — or ailing — members. They will thus do a fine work of charity and also provide new social contacts for themselves, along with the gratification of still being useful. In addition to friendly visiting, some ladies could offer to do some of the housework for the sick and cook meals for them. The men could do other chores for the incapacitated.

Such services could be a blessing for the less able and save them and the community much money. And those who perform the services would get themselves numbered among the Good Samaritans. I feel that there is no excuse for able elderly people nor younger ones to feel lonely or unwanted or unnecessary. All they need is a sincere willingness to help others — the less fortunate. There is no limit to the works of mercy that need doing. Some of the services may be the kind for which some modest pay is possible — leaving both those who pay and those who receive ahead.

In addition to belonging to organizations specifically for the old, senior citizens, especially those still hale and hearty, owe it to themselves and the community to share in some of the humanitarian, cultural, even political efforts of the world.

Since in a political country like ours both the most good and the most harm comes from government, those of us in the later years should not only keep voting but should also show an active interest in political affairs. We should know our ward, county, state parties and leaders, and should use our little influence for what is best.

As for societies and organizations, the myriads of them, one can say that the more edifying and valuable they are, the more they are in need of support and membership. Race tracks are ever popular and taverns seldom go bankrupt. But a foreign mission society, an historical museum, a poetry club — these have a hard time of it. We do the most good if we support the most noble and dedicated activities for which we can generate interest. If we like both jazz and opera, then, since a thousand will hear jazz for one who will enjoy opera, we should throw in our lot with opera. Since thousands can play bingo for one who has the brains for chess, we should, if we can, sacrifice the bingo and promote chess. It is a good thing for the Irish, the Germans, the Polish, the Italians to form clubs to preserve their native dances and cooking; but since virtually everybody will support such clubs, then, if we happen to have the greater gift of appreciating good literature, we would do more good if we promoted clubs for Irish, German, Italian, Polish literature. If we can write poetry, let us not settle only for basket weaving. If we can enjoy the classics, let us rather organize a small reading circle than a large bridge club. Twenty members of a good book club are more significant in the world than a thousand bridge players!

I am interested in a just peace. I belong to several organizations which try to promote a just international order and to resist communism. How grateful the few of us interested in such idealistic efforts are for anyone, young or old, who is willing to join and help! The world needs everybody who has the capacity for supporting something noble and idealistic. The young seldom have the time or the inclination to support anything that holds out no promise of either romance or money. It is the women after forty and the man after sixty-five on whom one must lean to get the cultural and public spirited work of the world done.

The many Catholic organizations like the Council of Catholic Men, the Holy Name Society, the Confraternity of Christian Doctrine, Foreign Missions, parish credit unions, Knights of Columbus, Kolping Society, the Social Justice Union — their feminine counterparts — while they exist for us, they also need our support. Many of them would be happy to use capable older persons as treasurers and corresponding or recording secretaries. They could use those who have leadership qualities and are good speakers as chairmen and committee heads. They could especially use those with journalistic talents for publicity work. Catholics deserve the best publicity in the world but get the worst — largely because they lack trained or willing news writers and photographers. Everywhere senior citizens can help.

Father Clarence D. White, of the St. Louis Archdiocesan Council of Catholic Men, in "Senior Social Action," a splendid outline for such action, writes:

> We should look upon the aged . . . as a group having a wealth of time and talent, wisdom and experience which the Church can use in a special way. They are a potentially great source of manpower for Catholic Action. We need lay apostles. What better material for the lay apostolate is there than those who through a long life have fought "the good fight" and who are getting ready to make a final accounting.

The Church and the community, anxious to help the aged, also need the help of senior citizens in manifold ways. The world always has more than enough to do, though not often enough money to pay for it. That is especially true of really good works, of works which promote the Kingdom of God on earth: most needed in the world, for example, are foreign missions, yet they seem to get the fewest bequests! Those in the later years, whom society is probably paying at least a modest pension, can enrich their lives and make the world better by volunteering for some of this work or doing it at nominal wages.

When we volunteer for anything, we must make sure to do it just as efficiently as if we were on a high salary. Some tasks may well be done slowly, but never sloppily. And we should accept our assignments graciously and smilingly, as if we were glad of the chance. St. Francis and his Friars went about thankful for the chance to help the poor, the sinful, and the sick. Nor should we expect special commendation for our work; when however praise is offered, we should accept it modestly. And when work is done for us or under our direction, we should go out of our way to show appreciation. Being an active senior citizen will involve participation in many meetings and on many committees — it will mean talking from the floor or from the chair. Any public speaker, especially elder ones, do well to observe certain rules and cautions. We set them down as follows:

> We should make sure that we know what the whole thing is about. Sometimes, perhaps owing to faulty hearing, oldsters get off on a tangent to the pity or despair of the hearers.
> We should never talk longer than the circumstances warrant. No matter how important we consider our contribution, we should rather have our tongue clipped than talk too long — one of the worst temptations of elder citizens.
> We should not reminisce, or dwell on the good old days, unless specifically invited to do so; instead, we should stick scrupulously to the point, logically and factually.
> We should not sound opinionated or as if our view should be adopted simply because we are older and have more experience. Let our facts and figures speak, not our ego.
> We should talk as loud as is necessary and try to look at our audience as directly as we can.
> Finally, we should always talk genially, graciously, never irritably or sourly. Let us differ, if we must, courteously, and so show those up as wrong who think oldsters are necessarily cantankerous and hypercritical.

To be an elder citizen rather than merely a senior one, our most important quality must be that we are wise, informed, and right. We should not throw ill-considered opinions around. Since the mere fact that we are supposedly old and wise may cause people to follow our advice uncritically, we must make doubly certain that it is good and right. We should read the best things we can, reflect on them, and then advise cautiously. Sometimes a whole career is affected by an elder's advice. Fortunes have been made and lost on the casual stock-market advice of someone! We should with fear and trembling express such opinions. An elder citizen should be noted for the careful thought behind ideas and expressions, not for his liberality in expressing them. Such an elder citizen is a blessing to his family, friends, Church, and community, and he will be honored and welcomed accordingly.

CHAPTER XIV

Keeping an Eye on the Next World

ONE can biologize or psychologize about the later years however one likes, the essence of the matter remains that old age makes real sense only if recognized as a spiritual ripening. The later years give the human personality the opportunity to develop its spiritual potentialities to the full. They downgrade "the flesh," and upgrade the spirit, so that we can more easily make it bright and shining for our meeting with our Maker.

To the natural man, old age can only be a time of shriveling and infirmity, foreboding the final and painful demise. Only to the spiritual man is it a bonus time of high enterprise, the exciting last lap of the race to the eternal goal for which the whole performance from the cradle to the grave should have been a striving. The more we supplant the natural man with the spiritual one, the more adjusted and satisfying the later years will be. For the saints, who ardently and truly longed to join the heavenly host, for such saintly giants as St. Francis and St. Clare, the later years, even when wrapped in pain and suffering, were welcome as signaling their approaching admission into eternal glory.

However, since few of us are saints and most of us remain tenaciously wrapped in the flesh — the loves, hates, and appetites of this world — our later years, like all the previous ones, continue to be a tug of war between what our body craves and our soul yearns for. Probably the mere recognition of the nature of this struggle would improve our acceptance of the later years. At least it might keep us from blaming the wrong things for discontent: such as insufficient money, lack of friends, inattention of loved

ones, coldness of society. We might come to feel with Wordsworth, "Nuns fret not at their convent's narrow walls," and with
Lovelace, "Stone walls do not a prison make, / Nor iron bars a
cage; / Minds innocent and quiet take / That for an hermitage."

The realization that most of the unhappiness in the later years
stems from the large residue of the Old Adam in us will not of
course remove the residue magically. If it were that easy, everybody would be good and everybody would get to heaven. Whatever is worthwhile must be worked for and prayed for. But it
might help us accept many of the drawbacks of age as part of
the Divine plan and impel us to find consolation where only it
can finally be found — in God. The Scriptural words, "Thou
shalt keep him in perfect peace whose mind is stayed on Thee,"
are not idle rhetoric but the "gospel" truth. Unfortunately, wishing to stay our mind on God does not alone accomplish it. It
will generally have taken a lifetime of spiritual effort and of
sinlessness to achieve such contemplation. But we can at least
try hard to keep our mind on God in these later years.

Religion, if ever, should certainly in the later years dominate
our lives. Yet some surveys rather shockingly indicate that oldsters
do not noticeably turn to religion. These studies suggest that
as the twig was bent so grew the tree, those who were religious
when young are so when old, and the irreligious in youth remain
irreligious still. They seem to bear out the stark implications of
the parable of the wheat and the cockle. They were both suffered to grow until the harvest time, when first the cockle was
bound and burned, and then the wheat gathered into the barn
(Mt. 13:24–30). Those who are cockles in youth are not likely
to become wheat upon reaching sixty-five!

Delton L. Scudder, summing up a gerontological conference on
religion, wrote, "There is nothing in the Bible which indicates
that spirituality naturally and automatically increases with age."[1]
In fact, "The evidence is largely negative. People do not grow

---

[1] *Organized Religion and the Older Person.* A Report on the Eighth
Annual Southern Conference on Gerontology held at the University of
Florida, Apr. 10–11, 1958, University of Florida Press, Gainsville, 1958,
p. 105.

increasingly more religious as they become older." Dr. Ninal Kirkpatrick Covalt, in "The Meaning of Religion to Older People — The Medical Perspective," drawing on his own experience in Muncie, Indiana, declares:

> The remark has often been made that "people turn to religion as they grow older." In my own personal experience, I have not been aware of this fact. Neither have I known people to "turn to religion" when they are seriously ill, the victims of a catastrophic illness, or severely, even permanently, physically handicapped (see *ibid.*, p. 79).

In his experience, "People who were good in their youth, remain good; the stable family unit (with the exception of the occasional stray black sheep) tends to continue on that level through several generations" (p. 88). Milton L. Barron in "The Role of Religion and Religious Institutions in Creating the Milieu of Older People," denies the assumption "that, with increasing chronological age, religiosity increases," and states:

> Instead of a large-scale 'turning to religion' as people grow older, most people simply persist in the religious patterns of their earlier age-statuses (*Organized Religion*, p. 30).

He concludes that "The over-all picture that research provides is that religion plays a smaller part in the lives of older people than one would assume" (*op. cit.*, p. 18).

There is some evidence that this is unfortunately true also among Catholics. To the question, "Do you attend Church more/less often than you did five years ago?" asked in a survey of 437 parishioners over 60 of St. Philip Neri Parish in St. Louis, 63 did not answer, 219 said about the same, 95 said less often, and only 60 said more often.[2] To the same question put to old people in a survey of St. Boniface Parish, Buffalo, "Almost six in ten said they were attending Church about as frequently as they had five years earlier. . . . Three in ten were attending

---

[2] *Older People in the Family, the Parish and the Neighborhood.* A Study of St. Philip Neri Parish, St. Louis, Mo., Catholic Charities of St. Louis, 1955, p. 34. Of those who attended less often, 47 gave "Ill health or injury," as a mitigating reason, ten gave age, three distance. Eight admitted to being "Fallen away Catholics."

less frequently," and only some nine percent were attending more frequently.[3] Though about half of the group were regular communicants, one fourth weekly and one fourth monthly, "Slightly less than one in ten never received Communion." Some of Dr. Bower's conclusions are as follows:

> While their religion was an important element in the lives of the older people who made up the study group, the Church and the clergy did not play an active part in the everyday lives of most of them . . . the great majority did not take active part in the church's religious and social organization. Roughly a third had had to curtail even formal religious activities due to poor health. . . .

In *A Study of the Aging in a Cleveland Parish*, Sister Mary Therese, O.P., found the following:

> More than half of the persons we saw attend Mass every Sunday. . . . Nearly two-thirds of the older people attended church as frequently as they did five years ago. On the other hand, nearly one-fourth attended less often, while only a very small fraction attended more often. Men and older persons were represented in larger proportions in the "Attend less often than five years ago" category. . . . Only about one-fourth of the people like to participate in church organizations. . . .[4]

A study dealing predominantly with Catholics in Chicago found that 54 per cent of the subjects said "religion had become more helpful to them in the past ten years," 30 per cent said it had not, 6 per cent said it remained the same, and 9 per cent did not answer. The comment followed that "Church attendance, however, had not increased proportionately since the subjects became 65."[5]

---

[3] Janet Bower, Ph.D., *Older People of St. Boniface Parish*, Catholic Charities of Buffalo, N. Y., 1957, pp. 67–71. While two thirds of the respondents said that they had no difficulty in getting to church, nearly a third "declared that it was hard for them to get there."

[4] The National Conference of Catholic Charities, Washington 6, D. C., 1954, p. 17. "Reasons given for failure to participate in church services more frequently included poor health, work, lack of transportation and adverse weather conditions." From these various studies one gets the impression that more older people would go to Church more frequently if they were supplied with convenient transportation.

[5] Charles T. O'Reilly and Margaret M. Pembroke, *Older People in a Chicago Community*, Loyola University Press, Chicago, 1957, pp. 30–31.

In fact all studies reveal encouraging results to the question, "Do you find religion helpful?" According to Sister Mary Therese, "An overwhelming number, 80 per cent of the men and 91 per cent of the women, declared religion to be helpful in their daily lives and/or in times of stress. . . . In addition, religion seemed to be more helpful to those in poor health" (*op. cit.*, p. 16). Dr. Bower found that the respondents "took comfort from their religion and pride in supporting its established ways" (*op. cit.*, p. 67). The St. Louis study found the importance of religion to the aged "was particularly noticeable when they were confronted with life's greatest hazards including sickness and death" (*op. cit.*, p. 11). Other denominational studies found that the older people get the more they tend to think of themselves as religious, and most particularly does their belief in an afterlife increase after 60. Milton L. Barron reports that "there is a clear pattern of the increase in the proportion of affirmative belief in afterlife as one ascends the chronological ladder" (see *Organized Religion*, p. 26).

It is a general hypothesis "that churchgoing and positive religious attitudes are significantly correlated with old-age adjustments." While not all findings consistently support this hypothesis conclusively, "the Landis doctoral study of older rural people in Iowa found that on all scores those who attend church regularly are not only better adjusted but enjoy better health than those who do not attend" (see *Organized Religion*, p. 28).

But even if religion does not immediately or always give us great comfort, we must realize that only religion can give our later years value. We take medicine for the good of our body even if it does not always taste good or bring immediate relief. We must regard religion as the medicine of our souls. The less oldsters have practiced their religion in their youth and middle years, the more they need to do so in their later years to make up for lost spiritual time. But the less accustomed one is to spiritual exercises the more arduous one will find them at the beginning. Attending Mass, receiving the sacraments, saying the rosary, praying daily must not be expected to give us immediate consolation, and the newer we are to such devotions the less consolation they are likely to give us. We must rather do them as a duty, and expect some calluses for our efforts! Many people falsely imagine that for religion to do them any good they must enjoy it, they must get a warm glow of feeling from it. But not even the saints have always had the grace of deep spiritual joy as they prayed before the Cross.

Religion can supply the only solid philosophical foundation for a successful old age. Materialistically considered, the later years are a waning and an ebbing — of strength, of agility, of worldly opportunities. As Longfellow wrote of old age, "It is not strength but weakness." However, he rightly added, ". . . age is opportunity no less / Than youth itself, though in another dress. . . ." It takes a spiritual outlook to appreciate this other dress. It is not enough, like a pagan to be resigned to old age as something unavoidable. What is required for full adjustment is the acceptance of old age as the climax of life, the final victory of it. The really religious person must recognize that just as an apple that were perennially green would be a waste, that only the ripe apple plucked fulfills its destiny, so man in order to fulfill his destiny must develop the qualities of "a ripe old age." His destiny can only be the purification of his soul, the cleansing of earthly desires and lusts, the harmonizing of his will with God's to a point where when his body disintegrates, his soul can join the angels.

God has created the later years with precisely those factors which will make easier his spiritual regeneration. As Lawrence Sterne wrote, "God tempers the wind to the shorn lamb." The most important of these is that in the later years sex is much less of an urgency. The desire, the capacity, and opportunity imperceptibly but surely have declined. For the natural man and woman that is of course the sharpest of tragedies. It is no doubt the real cause of most of the derangements of age. But the saints spend a lifetime praying for just this decline of sexual temptation. Those pledged by vows to chastity spend a lifetime fasting to tame and control and blunt these impulses. One recalls that even a few wise pagans rejoiced that age had liberated them from the searing bondage of sex. Cicero wrote, "It was an excellent reply that Sophocles made to a certain man who asked him, when he was already old, if he still indulged in the delights of love. 'Heaven forbid!' he said. 'Indeed I have fled from them as from a harsh and cruel master.'"

Many of the other temptations of the younger years tend to be blunted. Cicero rejoiced that old age had increased his appetite "for conversation and removed that for food and drink." Pride, envy, and jealousy have little object. As to most things that once mattered so much, one feels like saying with Ecclesiastes, "Vanity of vanities, and all things are vanity." Ambition loses its spur when we begin to feel in our bones that the end of the road is the tomb.

But this very consciousness of the earthly futility of everything can also become a roadblock for any and all useful endeavor unless we are imbued with the proper Christian spirit. During the heyday of life one can be a pagan, yet, as Longfellow puts it, go on "still achieving, still pursuing" because of a variety of rewards: money, fame, power, and, in the words of Byron, "To see the bright eyes of the dear one discover / She thought that I was not unworthy to love her." But when all these possibilities are virtually vanished, why should one go on striving. Yet we must go on. Gordon Poteat in "The Ministry of Organized Religion to the Aged," writes:

> When one ceases to strive one begins to decline and deteriorate. We must have goals for living. Many people set goals for themselves which, when achieved, seem jejune. That is why many oldsters are bored with life. They are like the famous actor who declared: "What I thought I wanted I finally got, but then I found that I never should have sought it," or they are like the writer of Ecclesiastes, who concludes a recital of all that he sought and found: "It was a striving for the wind and vanity of vanities" (see *Organized Religion*, p. 49).

Religion offers an antidote to false value and dying motivation. Gordon Poteat writes, "Religion sets goals that are inexhaustible and unattainable, but because of that they call out enthusiasm

and self-sacrifice as long as one lives." Because religion makes
heaven our goal and keeps us aware that to deserve it we must
go on doing our best to make ourselves and the world better,
it gives us an undying motive for living creatively. Once when my
father in his sixties was planting fruit trees, I asked him why he
was doing it since he would not live to enjoy their bearing. He
answered unperturbed, "I may never see them bear, but when
I was growing up there were fruit trees, and I want to pay the
debt by leaving trees for those who come after me." Very many
of the things we plan and do in the later years must be based
not on personal profit but on altruism — on love of God and
neighbor. We must keep extending ourselves, doing what is good
and noble, not because it will pay off here, but in the hereafter.
To do this with enthusiasm and fervor is almost impossible
without a vivid faith in an afterlife, a fear of punishment and
a hope of reward after death. As one gray-haired widow said,
"The church does nothing for me about growing old but a lot
about staying young" (see *Organized Religion*, p. 52).

For a Christian who is rich in Faith the later years cannot
lack motivation for making amends for past sins and for becoming
more familiar with virtue and goodness. Mixed with anxiety for
his worthiness will be a growing confidence his prayers and
his Guardian Angel will bring him out all right. In *The
Brothers Karamazov*, Dostoevski has Father Zossima say truly and
beautifully:

> The mild serenity of age takes the place of the riotous blood
> of youth. I bless the rising sun each day and, as before, my heart
> sings to meet it, but now I love even more its setting, its long
> slanting rays and the soft, tender, gentle memories that come
> with them, the dear images from the whole of my long, happy
> life — and over all the Divine Truth, softening, reconciling, for-
> giving. My life is ending — I know that well — but every day that
> is left me I feel how my earthly life is in touch with a new in-
> finite, unknown, but approaching life, the nearness of which sets
> my soul quivering with rapture, my mind glowing and my heart
> weeping with joy (Modern Library edition, p. 360).

That expresses beautifully the only proper and creative way to live the later years. The saints live so — and the rest of us should try to do likewise. For Catholics it should not be too hard. We should find it comparatively easy to keep an eye on the next world. The Church offers us such a vast machinery of devotions, rituals, and sacraments, and the Holy Sacrifice of the Mass, that our souls might well quiver with anticipation of the life to come.

CHAPTER XV

A Brave and Christian Conclusion

FOR the natural man, life's two hardest compulsions are growing old and dying. The previous chapters have tried to create in us a Christian acceptance of growing old. This concluding chapter must try to condition us for that awesome climax of our lives when, as Louise Imogen Guiney in "Beati Mortui" wrote, "Man . . . divinely vernal / Storms into life eternal."

Long ago Cicero said that upon death "we should reflect from youth up, so that we may be indifferent to it." For a Christian, all of life should certainly be a conscious preparation for the awful moment when we must leave our body and render up our soul to our Maker to await the judgment of salvation or damnation. The blessing of the later years is that they give us longer to prepare for this moment under increasingly congenial circumstances. The proper Christian understanding tells us readily that the wrinkles and infirmities of age are not a curse but a series of meaningful *Memento Mori* along our way.

While for a pagan death is an intolerable thought, it is even for all but the most saintly Christian an awesome one. The saints, whose will is fully harmonious with God's, await death eagerly and glory in the thought of it. We, too, must be more than resigned to it, we must accept it as a crucial part of the Divine Will. Whatever compensations one may attribute to the later years, their awesomest note is that they have brought us to the point where the next stage is death. Nothing can soften that prospect except the belief in an afterlife and the hope of heaven. "Death," writes Friar Alfred Martin, "is the supreme fact of life, and a realistic facing up to it brings peace, not distress" (*Friar*, Jan., 1959).

Poets and mystics down the ages have grappled with the problem of death. In their elegies, poets have reminded us that perhaps those who died are better off than the living. Milton in "Lycidas" tells us to weep no more for the friend drowned young because in heaven he will surely be a protector of seafarers "good to all who wander in that perilous flood." Tennyson in *In Memoriam*, mourning his friend Arthur Hallam, sighs that such commonplace reasons as "Other friends remain," or "Loss is common to the race" are poor consolation. What finally consoles him is "That men may rise on stepping stones / Of their dead selves to higher things," and that his friend now "lives in God." Therefore, he cries, "I shall not lose thee tho' I die. . . . Dear heavenly friend, that canst not die / Mine, mine for ever, ever more."

The poets and mystics keep urging us to keep our own souls in readiness for the awesome day. In the old morality play, when Death taps him on the shoulder just as he is arranging a party, Everyman exclaims, "O Death, Thou comest when I had thee least in mind." When God grants us the later years, He helps us not to let death catch us unprovisioned. Samuel Johnson, in his last essay in the *Idler*, April, 1760, wrote:

> The secret horror of the last is inseparable from a thinking being, whose life is limited, and to whom death is dreadful. We always make a secret comparison between a part and the whole; the termination of any period of life reminds us that life itself has likewise its termination; when we have done any thing for the last time, we involuntarily reflect that a part of the days allotted us is past, and that as more is past, there is less remaining.

For the natural part of us that is a terrifying realization; for the immortal part of us that should be a joyous anticipation. The later days should, if we live them perfectly, bring us to the attitude of St. Francis of Assisi. When he learned from his doctor that he had only a few weeks to live, he added the last two stanzas to his "Canticle of the Sun":

> Praise be Thou, my Lord, / For our sister Death of the Body /
> From whom no living man can flee.
> Woe to those who die in mortal sin, / Blessed are they she
> finds in Thy most holy will / To whom the second death can
> do no harm.

The whole process of aging seems to be divinely calculated to
bring man to feel that death is a kindly sister that can do no
harm if only we are without mortal sin and attuned to God's
holy will. All the later years are a series of signposts to what St.
Bernard calls *Mors janua vitae* — "the gate of life." Epictetus
called death "bugbear," Bryon "sunset," Barrie "an awfully big
adventure," Johnson "kind Nature's signal to retreat," George
Eliot "the great Reconciler," and Young "the crown of life."

All our lives of course we should be mindful of the advice in
Deuteronomy (32:29): "O that they would be wise and would
understand, and would provide for their last end." Yet in the
prime of life it is hard to do so. During that prime we tend to
feel like Countee Cullen: "Yet fear I deeply, too, / Lest Death
should greet and claim me ere / I keep Life's rendezvous." It is
hard to be resigned to dying while there is still so much to enjoy
on the low level and to accomplish on the high. Southey in
Joan of Arc writes, "Death! to the happy thou art terrible; / But
how the wretched love to think of thee, / O thou true comforter."
In *Richard III*, when Lord Hastings cries, ". . . ere a fortnight
make me older/ I'll send some packing that yet think not on't,"
Sir William Catesby answers, " 'tis a vile thing to die, my gracious
lord, / When men are unprepar'd and look not for it" (Act
III, scene ii).

For the unregenerated man, death even in the later years
remains terrible. In *Measure for Measure*, Shakespeare writes,

> The weariest and most loathful worldly life
> That age, ache, penury, and imprisonment
> Can lay on nature, is a paradise
> To what we fear of death.

And our body in the best of us fights against death to the last
breath. Dr. Nila Kirkpatrick Covalt writes that even in the very

throes of death, we tend to fight more for survival than meditate upon our salvation:

> I recall no persons who, as they were dying, or knew they were dying, called out to God or audibly prayed. Usually these persons are exerting every bit of energy in a struggle to try to keep living (see *Organized Religion*, p. 87).

Even the most Christian of poets, Tennyson, in "Two Voices" recognizes the tenacity of our nature: "Whatever crazy sorrow saith, / No life that breathes with human breath / Has ever truly long'd for death."

This simply means that the time to condition ourselves for a noble and holy death is during the slow decline that God grants those who grow old. A good death is a gift and a grace. Lamb in *John Woodvil*, wrote, "Men die but once, and the opportunity / Of a noble death is not an everyday fortune. / It is a gift which noble spirits pray for." Noble spirits who have prayed for it many years can say with Lowell, "And Death is beautiful as feet of friend / Coming with welcome at our journey's end," and with Florence Earle Coates, "Death — Life's servitor and friend — the guide / That safely ferries us from shore to shore!" and with William Croswell Doane that "it is turning seed-corn into grain, . . . winning Heaven's eternal gain, . . . freedom evermore from pain."

These poetic efforts to reconcile us to dying, even to welcome it as a release from earthly bondage and a ticket to eternal life are not just rhetoric. They are for the Christian the solemn truth. The later years can only be made happy and creative, despite any number of possible miseries, through the acceptance of this philosophy of death. Longfellow better than any other poet indicates poetically how God in His kindness has given us the later years with all their seeming losses and trials to facilitate our acceptance of death. In "Nature" he wrote:

> So Nature deals with us, and takes away
> Our playthings one by one, and by the hand
> Leads us to rest so gently, that we go
> Scarce knowing if we wish to go or stay. . .

Our playthings one by one are taken away: early our athletic prowess; then our romantic charms — along with perhaps some of our teeth, most of our hair, sharpness of vision and of hearing; then with retirement, our professional and economic powers; and finally some of our health.

Perhaps even more poignant and dramatic than these gradual losses are the funeral processions of our friends and relatives. We can hardly reach the later years without having often stood around a bier and heard the Church's solemn "Requiem aeternam dona ei, Domine: et lux perpetua luceat ei." Many of us may feel like crying with Lamb, "All, all are gone, the old familiar faces." As each beloved or familiar face passes away, we have somewhat less to live for here and more to go to there. Francis Thomson wrote, "As those we love decay, we die in part; / String after string is severed from the heart." Thomas Moore in "The Last Rose of Summer" sings, "Oh, who would inhabit / This bleak world alone!"

While it is important for our normality in the later years to keep trying to make new friends, we may nevertheless feel that those who died before us signaled our own terminal adventure and constitute a reception committee for us when we arrive on the other shore. To this effect Holmes wrote pertinently:

> Fast as the rolling seasons bring / The hour of fate to those we love, /
> Each pearl that leaves the broken string / Is set in Friendship's crown above. /
> As narrower grows the earthly chain, / The circle widens in the sky; /
> These are our treasures that remain, / But those are stars that beam on high.

Another poet, Nancy P. Wakefield, sings, "Over the river they beckon to me, / Loved ones who've cross'd to the farther side." As grandparents, parents, other relatives and friends "join the heavenly caravan" we begin to cling just a little less passionately to the lonely earth and dream more and more of those beyond.

But what physical and economic decline, and the passing away of dear ones cannot fully accomplish, that is all too often and surely done by sickness and pain. Pain is both the greatest terror of the later years and the most wonderful therapeutic.

For me most of my life as perhaps for many people the fear of pain was much worse than the fear of death. I used to pray to be spared pain, whatever else might be visited upon me. Only after seeing the effect of pain and suffering on my father during seven cancer operations in the last three years before his death at eighty, did I realize the spiritual beneficence pain can bring. During those years of suffering, my father turned more and more inward. The rosary became his most treasured possession. Though his body clung tenaciously to life, in pain he became resigned to death and begged God for it. When it came, one could not but feel that he was ready for it.

Seeing the effect of pain on him and on all of us who knew him gave me an entirely new and Christianized conception of pain. When my time of suffering comes, I hope it will stand me in good stead. It made it possible for me to appreciate the words on St. Joseph's Day, March 10, 1959, of the Holy Father, Pope John XXIII, to 6000 infirm people, many on stretchers, before him in the Basilica of St. Peter's. He said:

> Unfortunately many are led to consider all physical misfortunes in this world as evils, absolute evils. They have forgotten that pain is the inheritance of Adam's children. They have forgotten that the only real evil is sin, which offends the Lord, and that we must look at the Cross of Jesus in the same way as did the apostles, martyrs and saints, the masters and witnesses of the fact that in the Cross lies comfort and salvation and that one does not live without pain in the love of Christ.

The Holy Father went on to urge those afflicted not to "rebel under the weight of pain" to "understand the meaning of suffering," and to "realize the possibilities they have of contributing to the salvation of the world," to accept therefore "their life of pain in the same way as did Jesus Christ" (see *Brooklyn Tablet*, Mar. 28, 1959).

In art and literature, it has long been taken for granted that, as Shelley said of Byron, "Most wretched men / Are cradled into poetry by wrong: They learn in suffering what they teach in song." We read that Dante's tears, "hate of wrong," and "soul in pain" inspired the "medieval miracle of song," the Divine Comedy.

If suffering was necessary to inspire a "miracle of song," we should consider it likely to be necessary also to fashion an angelic soul. If in our later years God should choose to let us be visited with pain, let us not feel rebellious; let us rather recognize it as a means for our purification and pray for the strength to bear it. Let us say with Jesus, "My Father, if it be possible, let this chalice pass from me. Nevertheless not as I will, but as Thou wilt" (Mt. 26:39).

During a Good Friday Retreat (Elkins Park, Mar. 27, 1959), Father John C. McFadden, Director of the Catholic Information Center, Philadelphia, conducted a special conference on pain. "More crimes are committed in order to avoid pain," he said, "than for any other reason. . . . But pain will always be with us — the call is not to get rid of it but to know what to do with it. . . . Christ made it the very instrument of our salvation."

Father McFadden went on to say that of course, "We should try to ease the burden of pain — but there comes a point when there is nothing left but to take it. . . . The supremest lesson Our Lord taught us on earth is what to do with pain." He acknowledged that it is "difficult to accept God's permissive will in allowing pain." While we may be suffering for our own sins, it might also be for the sins of others, perhaps of our own family, or associates. "Unless we have the spirit of God's redemptive act of Good Friday," he concluded, "We can never understand the suffering we have because of the sins of others." But whether for ourselves or for others, most of us, he said, will eventually "like our Lord lie on our own hard bed of pain."

If it should be our lot that pain rack our later years, let us pray, and ask our relatives, friends, our pastor to pray that we be strong enough and brave enough to bear it for His sake, who suffered so much on the cross for us. Perhaps it will help us to recall that those whom God especially loves he seems to shower with pain. We think of the many martyrs; we think of those saintly beings who are given stigmata. We read that only persons who "practice the most heroic virtues and have a great love of the cross" receive the stigmata and that these "are preceded and accompanied by very severe suffering, physical and moral, which renders the subject conformable to Jesus' suffering" ("Stigmata," *Catholic Encyclopedia Dictionary*). These martyrs and saints, even when the pain is most excruciating, glory in their suffering, are spiritually happy in it because it is for Jesus' sake.

If they who are saintly glady suffer so much, then surely we, who even if we avoided mortal sins have a long roll of venial ones, should be chivalrous enough to take what pain is destined for us. Father Karl Adam, in *Christ Our Brother*, wrote:

> . . . our Lord himself drank the chalice of suffering to the dregs, a chalice full of physical and mental agony. From His Cross here streams a heavenly radiance, a golden light, upon all those thousands of sick and dying who daily climb the hill of Calvary . . . every second sees a man die. So death is not a rare and extraordinary thing, but a thing that is happening every day and hour and moment. Our life is a constant dying. The ancients were terrified by the inescapable nature of death; but Jesus banished that terror. For death is no longer the power that plunges the torch of life to extinction, but one that makes it shine more brightly for eternal life (Macmillan, 1938, pp. 108–109).

Sentiments like that can help us bear up under what sufferings the later years and the shadow of death may bring. With Christian conviction we can then say with the Psalmist, "For though I should walk in the midst of the shadow of death, I will fear no evils, for thou are with me" (Ps. 22:4).

Let us most of all rely on the consolations Holy Mother the Church can give us — confession, Communion, and extreme unction. Let us keep thanking God that He gave us so many later years to take advantage of the spiritual riches of the Church and prepare ourselves with prayers and sacraments for the final hour. When Father Daniel Lord, S.J., former editor of *The Queen's Work*, was told at 65 that he had incurable cancer of the lung, he answered bravely and wisely, "You're going to die sometime anyway. Something like this just makes it seem a little more definite" (*Newsweek*, Jan. 24, 1955). When a year later at 66 he did die, we can be sure that he had used that year of warning to the full for giving his soul the finishing spiritual touches. Those who loved him and were left behind could feel confident that when they sang with the Church, "Suscipiat te Christus qui vocavit te, et in sinum Abrahae Angeli deducant te," the Lord had indeed given him eternal rest and was letting perpetual light shine upon him!

When that shall be sung over us and if it can be sung confidently, then only have we fulfilled the purpose of our later years successfully. At the moment that our relatives and the Church sing the *Requiem* over us, may the angels in heaven and our friends gone before us sing our welcome into heaven!

And may this book have contributed a little to ensure this holy conclusion.

Bibliography

(Books, pamphlets, and articles used
and referred to more than incidentally)

Aging is Everyone's Concern (pa.), The Proceedings of the First
Ontario Conference on Aging (Toronto: University of Toronto,
1957).

Aging of Populations and Its Economic and Social Implications (pa.),
Population Studies, No. 26 (New York: United Nations, 1956).

Antrim, Doran K., "Start Again at 65," Catholic Digest, July, 1957.

App, Ph.D., Austin J., "The Catholic Stake in the Aged" Social
Justice Review, January, 1959; "Sands of Gold," Magnificat,
January, 1959.

Arthur, Julietta K., How to Help Older People (Philadelphia: H. B.
Lippincott, 1954).

Beckman, R. O., Health Examinations for Longer Life (pa.) (New
York: The Senior Service Foundation, 1957).

Boas, M.D., Ernst, Add Life to Your Years (New York: The
McBride Co., 1954).

Bortz, M.D., Edward L., Growth and Aging (pa.) (Devon, Pa.:
Devereaux Schools, 1957).

Bowen, Georgene E., "Salient Points on Organization of Clubs for
Older People" (mimeographed), Philadelphia: Health and Welfare Council, February, 1956.

Bower, Ph.D., Janet, Older People of St. Boniface Parish (pa.)
(Buffalo: Catholic Charities of Buffalo, 1957).

Brophy, Liam, "Old Age is Worth Waiting For," Apostle, November, 1958.

Cicero, On Old Age, trans. by Moses Hadas (New York: Modern
Library, 1951).

Claudel, Paul, "Old Age According to Sacred Scripture," trans. by
Msgr. P. J. Doyle, P.P., The Irish Ecclesiastical Review, October,
1946.

Colby, Anita, "So I'm an Old Maid," Sign, November, 1954.

Corson, John J., and John W. McConnell, Economic Needs of
Older People (New York: The Twentieth Century Fund, 1956).

Crampton, M.D., C. Ward, Live Long and Like It (New York:
Public Affairs Pamphlet No. 139, 4th ed., 1956).

Current Population Reports (Washington, D. C.: Bureau of the Census), December 18, 1957; March 19, 1958; and November 10, 1958.

Donahue, Wilma, editor, *Free Time: Challenge to Later Maturity* (Ann Arbor: University of Michigan Press, 1958).

Doyle, Kathleen, *When Mental Illness Strikes Your Family* (New York: Public Affairs Pamphlet No. 172, July, 1956).

Drake, Prof. Joseph T., *The Aged in American Society* (New York: Ronald Press, 1958).

Fecher, Ph.D., Constantine J., *The Longevity of Members of Catholic Sisterhoods* (diss.) (Washington, D. C.: The Catholic University, 1927).

Gibson, John E., "How to Stay Young," *Catholic Digest*, May, 1957.

Good News for Later Life (pa.) (New York: State Joint Legislative Committee on Problems of Aging, 1958).

"'Gradual Retirement' — Latest Idea for Older Workers," *U.S. News*, September 26, 1958.

Green, Paul, "How Long Will You Live," *Catholic Digest*, January, 1953.

Greer, S.D.B., Brother Jack, "Those of the Eleventh Hour," *Catholic School Journal*, March, 1955.

Groene, Theodore, *How to Enjoy Retirement for the Rest of Your Life* (New York: Exposition Press, 1957).

Guardini, Rev. Romano, "Am Abend des Lebens" (mimeographed), Munich, Germany: Frauenfunk (Radio), December 28, 1956.

Gunther, Max, "A Vitality Diet for a Young Middle Age," *Coronet*, December, 1958.

Hamilton, Mrs. Clara H., *Your Rewarding Years* (New York: Bobbs-Merrill, 1955).

Hart, S.J., Robert, and Paul P. Harbrecht, S.J., "Status of the Aged," *Social Order*, March, 1958.

Health Guide for Institutions Serving Older People (pa.) (Philadelphia: Health and Welfare Council, 1958).

Housing the Elderly (pa.) (Washington, D. C.: Housing and Home Finance Agency, April, 1959).

Housing Requirements of the Aged (pa.), Housing Research Center (Ithaca, N. Y.: Cornell University, November, 1958).

Informal Educational Opportunities for Older People in the Philadelphia Area (pa.) (Philadelphia: Health and Welfare Council, September, 1958).

Johnson, Dr. Harry J., "How to Retire and be Happy" (interview), *U. S. News*, February 1, 1957.

Kempfer, Homer, *Education for a Long and Useful Life* (pa.), Bulletin 1950, No. 6 (Washington, D. C.: U. S. Department of Health, Education and Welfare, Reprint, 1954).

Lawton, George, and Maxwell S. Stewart, *When You Grow Older*

(New York: Public Affairs Pamphlet No. 131, 14th ed., October, 1956).

Linden, M.D., Maurice E., "Don't be Afraid to Grow Old" (leaflet, 1954); "A New Way to Help Old People" (leaflet, n.d.); "The Challenge of the Geriatric Patient" (pamphlet, 1952); "The Promise of Therapy in the Emotional Problems of Aging" (mimeographed, 1957), all of these, Philadelphia: Division of Mental Health.

Martin, Fr. Alfred, "The Golden Years: From Fifty to Seventy," *Friar*, October, 1958; "And Beyond That: Labor and Pain," *Friar*, January, 1959.

McDonough, C.P., Rev. Aloysius, "Late Vocations," *Sign*, November, 1954.

Neisser, Edith G., *How to be a Good Mother-in-law and Grandmother* (New York: Public Affairs Pamphlet No. 174, July, 1956).

Ogg, Elizabeth, *When Parents Grow Old* (New York: Public Affairs Pamphlet No. 208, June, 1954); *Why Some Women Stay Single*, ibid., Pamphlet No. 177, 1951.

Older People in the Family, the Parish and the Neighborhood (pa.) (St. Louis: Catholic Charities of St. Louis, 1955).

Older Person in the Home, The (pa.), Public Health Service Publication No. 542 (Washington, D. C.: U. S. Department of Health, Education, and Welfare, 1957).

O'Reilly, Charles T., and Margaret M. Pembroke, *Older People in a Chicago Community* (pa.) (Chicago: Loyola University, 1957).

"The Pension Society," *The Wall Street Journal*, June 9, 1959.

Pollack, Jack Harrison, "The Older the Smarter," *Catholic Digest*, April, 1959.

Rudd, Dr. T. N., *The Nursing of the Elderly Sick* (Philadelphia: J. B. Lippincott, 1954).

Scudder, Delton L., editor, *Organized Religion and the Older Person* (pa.) (Gainsville: University of Florida Press, 1958).

Shock, Dr. Nathan W., *Trends in Gerontology*, 2nd ed. (Stanford, Calif.: Stanford University Press, 1957); "Can You Stay Young Longer?" (interview), *U. S. News*, October 23, 1953.

Sister Mary Therese, O.P., *A Study of the Aging in a Cleveland Parish* (pa.) (Washington, D. C.: National Conference of Catholic Charities, 1954).

Smaridge, Norah, "How to Be a Good Aunt," *Ave Maria*, June 28, 1958.

Spence, Hartzell, "Parsons-Come-Lately," *Saturday Evening Post*, August 29, 1959.

Standards of Care for Older People in Institutions, Section I (New York: National Committee on the Aging, of the National Social Welfare Assembly, 1953).

Statistical Bulletin (pa.) (New York: Metropolitan Life Insurance Co.), November, 1957; March, 1958; April, 1958; June, 1958.

Steincrohn, M.D., Peter J., *Live Longer and Enjoy It!* (Englewood Cliffs, N. J.: Prentice Hall, 1956).

Stieglitz, M.D., Edward J., *The Second Forty Years* (Philadelphia: J. B. Lippincott, 1952); "Do You Want to Live Longer?" (interview), *U. S. News*, February 14, 1958.

Terhune, M.D., William B., *Harvest Years* (pa.) (New Haven, Conn.: The Silver Hill Foundation, 1954).

Tompkins, Dorothy C., *The Senile Aged Problem in the United States* (pa.) (Berkeley, Calif.: Bureau of Public Administration, University of California, January, 1955).

Turkel, Roma Rudd, *Day After Tomorrow* (New York: P. J. Kenedy & Sons, 1956).

Wuermeling, Dr. Franz-Josef, "Alarming Population Trends," *Bulletin*, Bonn, Germany, October 18, 1956.

Index

175